Gemini Predictions and Rituals 2025

Alina Rubi

Published Independently

All Rights Reserved © 2025.

Astrologers: Alina Rubí

Editing: Alina A. Rubi and Angeline A. Rubi

rubiediciones29@gmail.com

No part of this 2025 yearbook may be reproduced or transmitted in any form or by any electronic or mechanical means. Including photocopying, recording, or any other system of archiving and retrieving information, without the prior written permission of the author.

Who is Gemini?	9
Gemini Personality	10
Gemini General Horoscope	12
Love	13
Economy	14
Gemini Health	16
Important Dates	16
Gemini Monthly Horoscopes 2025	18
January 2025	18
February 2025	20
March 2025	22
April 2025	24
May 2025	26
June 2025	28
July 2025	30
Lucky Numbers	31
August 2025	32
September 2025	34
Lucky Numbers	35
October 2025	36
Lucky Numbers	37
November 2025	38
December 2025	40
Lucky Numbers	41
The Tarot Cards, an Enigmatic and Psychological World.	42

The Star, Tarot Card for Gemini 2025 45
Lucky Colors 46
    Gemini 48
Lucky Charms 49
Lucky Quartz for 2025 52
    Lucky Quartz Gemini /2025 56
Compatibility of Gemini and the Zodiac Signs 57
Best Professions 67
Stress. An obstacle on the road to 2025 68
Digital Narcissism 71
The Moon in Gemini 75
The importance of the Rising Sign 76
Ascendant in Gemini 81
    Aries – Ascendant Gemini 82
    Taurus – Ascendant Gemini 82
    Gemini – Ascendant Gemini 83
    Cancer – Gemini Ascendant 84
    Leo – Ascendant Gemini 84
    Virgo – Ascendant Gemini 85
    Libra – Gemini Ascendant 85
    Scorpio – Gemini Ascendant 86
    Sagittarius– Ascendant Gemini 86
    Capricorn – Ascendant Gemini 87
    Aquarius – Gemini Ascendant 88
    Pisces – Ascendant Gemini 88
Energy Cords 89

Evil Eye, Curses and Envy	97
Psychic Possessions	98
Lucky dates to get married in 2025:	99
Lucky Days for Rituals 2025	99
Lunar Calendar 2025	105
Full Moon Calendar 2025	117
Energy Cleanses by 2025	118
Bath to Open Your Paths 2025	118
Lucky Bath	119
Blockage's Removal Bath	119
Bath to Attract Harmony in the Home	119
Bath Against Envy	120
Bath against Negativity	120
Bath to Attract Money	121
Curse Bath	122
Aphrodisiac bath	122
Beauty Bath	123
Bath to Restore Energies and Vitality	124
Bath to Attract Love	124
Bath to Get Fast Money	125
Bath for Material Prosperity	125
Bath for Spiritual Peace	126
Bath for Protection against Envy	126
Bath to Attract Success	127
Bath for Instant Luck	128
Bath for Good Luck	128

Bath to Be Attractive 130

Bath to Recover a Love... 130

Bath to Eliminate the Evil Eye 131

Bath to Attract Abundance 131

Rituals for January 133

Ritual for money 133

Spell for good energies and prosperity....................................... 134

Ritual for Love 135

Spell to Make Someone Think of You 136

Spell to Preserve Good Health 137

Rituals for February 139

Ritual with Honey to Attract Prosperity..................................... 139

To Attract Impossible Love 140

Ritual for Health 141

Rituals for March 143

Ritual with Oil for Love 144

Spell to improve health 144

Rituals for April 146

Ritual for love 147

Spell against Depression 148

African Aphrodisiac 148

Mint 149

Garlic 150

Rituals for May 152

Spell to Attract Your Soulmate 153

Ritual for Health 154

Rituals for June 155
Ritual to Attract More Money. 155
Ritual to Consolidate Love 156
Rituals for July 158
Romani Ritual 159
Bath for Good Health 159
Rituals for August 161
Ritual for Money 161
Spell to Transform you into a Magnet 162
Bath for Health 162
Bamboo 163
Pumpkin 163
Eucalyptus 164
Parsley 165
Laurel 166
Rituals for September 167
Love Spell with Basil and Red Coral 167
Ritual for Health 168
Rituals for October 169
Ritual to Ensure Prosperity 169
Spell to Subdue in Love 170
Bath with Parsley for Health. 170
Energy Cleansing with an Egg 171
Rituals for November 174
Ritual for the Union of Two Persons 175
Shamanic Energy Cleansing 176

Rituals for December 178
Cash Flow Ritual 178
About The Authors 179

Who is Gemini?

Dates: May 21 - June 21

Day: Wednesday

Color: Blue

Element: Air

Compatibility: Libra, Aries, and Aquarius

Symbol: ♊

Modality: Mutable

Polarity: Male

Ruling Planet: Mercury

House: 3

Metal: Mercurio

Quartz: Crystal, beryl, and topaz.

Constellation: Gemini

Gemini Personality

Gemini has great adaptability and versatility, they are intellectual, eloquent, affectionate, and intelligent. They have a lot of energy and vitality, they love to talk, read, do several things at the same time.

This is a sign that enjoys the unusual and novelty, the more variety in their life, the better. Its character is double and complex, sometimes contradictory. On the one hand, it is versatile, but on the other it can be dishonest.

Gemini is the sign of twins and, as such, their character and way of being is dual. They represent contradiction, and they change their minds or moods easily.

Geminis are continually active and need to always be busy, they love to multitask and try new challenges.

They have the happiness, imagination, creativity, and restlessness of children. Some start new activities and challenges with enthusiasm, but often lack the perseverance to finish them. From their point of view, life is a game, and they are looking for fun and new experiences. Gemini is the most childish sign of the zodiac.

Their good humor and communication skills disappear when they are faced with a problem, as they tend to get discouraged in the worst circumstances and let others look for solutions.

Geminis are highly intelligent, they ask everything. This makes them masters of debate. It is one of the signs with the highest IQ.

Gemini General Horoscope

This will be a promising year for Gemini. However, occasionally some obstacles will appear in their path, especially in the periods of Mercury retrograde.

You must adapt to changes and accept challenges because you will receive many rewards. You must tie up the loose ends of your life and focus on opportunities to expand your horizons, find new interests, and connect with others.

Gemini will have many passionate encounters throughout the year, and their income will increase. Remember that there are no gains in life without sacrifices. Be patient with your relationships and trust your inner self for strength and positive vibes.

The planetary events of 2025 will set the stage for a year full of dynamic change and opportunities for growth. The purpose of these events is to push you to let go of outdated patterns and embrace new possibilities.

There are many transits that promise you abundance, and a renewed sense of optimism and confidence. This is an excellent time to focus on broadening your horizons, whether it is through travel, education, or exploring new ideas.

The year will not be without challenges and will test your ability to think, but it will also offer you valuable lessons in patience and perseverance.

Jupiter will remain in your sign until June 9, 2025, so you can continue to enjoy the blessings of this transit.

During New Moon periods seek out new experiences, initiate new projects, and focus on your own wants and needs. Take good care of yourself, and make sure you do things the right way, and for the right reasons.

Love

Geminis who are engaged will deepen the emotional connection with their partner. Lunar Eclipses will cause changes, or necessary adjustments, in the dynamics of the relationship. This can lead to a more fulfilling relationship.

Singles get ready to embrace their playful side as the transit of Jupiter through your sign will amplify their magnetism, making it easier to attract potential partners who appreciate your intelligence and adventurous spirit.

This year will be a period of sentimental changes for Gemini, they will make plans to have children and to improve their bonds. The periods of Eclipses will be times of beginnings and endings in relationships. There are many other aspects that ensure that there will be a lot of passion in your romantic relationships.

This year could open new doors and bring new suitors into your life, although it will also be a period of self-reflection.

Throughout the year, they will see better chemistry with their partners, and they will be able to express their opinions freely.

During the Full Moon periods, emotions will be strong in your love connections, and you may want to spend more time with those with whom you have a good connection. You may want to improve love relationships that are unstable.

This year you will have extra energy for love, and romance, and if you are single, you will be showered with dates. If you are in a relationship, you will want to rekindle the sparks and make it feel like the first time.

New Moons will renew your romantic relationships, and periods of Mercury retrograde can bring up problems.

Economy

2025 will be a big year for Gemini in business, agreements, and exposure of ideas. Particularly those who are dedicated to communication businesses will do well. He would come up with new ideas that can be put into practice thanks to technology. You should try to make connections and look for new opportunities. Some might land their dream job, but it is important that they do not compromise beyond their means. All your efforts will be recognized and rewarded.

Embrace change and look for new opportunities for financial expansion. The transit of Jupiter will bring you opportunities for your career advancement, and more streams of income. If you have been considering having your own business, the cosmic energies will support your efforts. However, it is crucial that you adapt to the circumstances. Your flexibility and quickness of thought will serve you well during this period. The year promises you abundance, it is an ideal time to diversify your investments, explore new sources of income or invest in your professional development.

Neptune and Saturn will cause you to focus on your goals, which you connect with spiritually, and allow you to help others. During New Moon periods you can feel energized and maximize your resources. During Full Moon periods try to focus, be more confident, and maximize good energy for your goals.

You may struggle to progress, discipline, and focus on Mercury Retrograde periods and may be insecure, or lacking confidence.

This year you will have new job opportunities, and you may be presented with opportunities even if you are not looking for a new job.

Gemini Health

During the eclipse seasons you will receive orders from your doctor to change your lifestyle. Remember that discipline does not have to feel like punishment. Use your willpower while reducing your addiction to sugar, coffee, or another stimulant that simply is not good for your body.

You must nourish yourself physically and emotionally, and reevaluate your lifestyle, it is essential that you stay away from stress and anxiety. Emotional stress, compounded, can cause your immune system to be affected.

If you are dealing with an addiction, find the courage to seek help or go into detox.

Important Dates

February 4 - End of Jupiter retrograde.

May 20 - Entry of the Sun into Gemini

May 26 – Entry of Mercury into Gemini

May 27 - New Moon in Gemini

July 4 - Venus Entry into Gemini

July 9 – Uranus enters Gemini.

September 6 - Uranus retrograde.

December 4 - Full Moon in Gemini

Gemini Monthly Horoscopes 2025

January 2025

This month, in the economy, it is essential that you exercise prudence. You may be faced with people who want to take advantage of your gullibility. You cannot trust just anyone without knowing them, you will have to be with your five senses wide awake to avoid a lot of trouble.

If you are in a relationship, you will try to overcome your conflicts by implementing alternative solutions, including resolving your worries in someone else's arms.

If you do not have a partner, analyzing the real reasons, and stop blaming your failures on the people you have dated, is a good idea. If you analyze things carefully, the common factor in all these disagreements is you.

After the 19th, the economic area in your relationship needs prudence, talk extensively with a financial advisor before starting any investment.

Do not settle for advice you may have heard in the past, as the information you may have heard could be misleading.

At the end of the month, if you do not have a partner, you will finally understand that the main cause of your loneliness is none other than you.

If you want to change course, and take charge of your life you must act, it is the best way to achieve it.

Luckily, the people around you will make you understand that fantasizing is allowed, but taking action and turning your dreams into reality is much better.

Lucky Numbers

10, 24, 28, 30, 33

February 2025

This month you will dream so much of changing your life.

You must make decisions and change your way of proceeding so as not to make the same mistakes again. Do not expect solutions to come from other people, or external sources. If you are not satisfied with your current situation, it is in your hands to change it.

Do not think that a fairy godmother is going to appear and change your life, you must take the frying pan by the handle to transform your situation. No one can do it for you, you are the one who holds the key to your happiness.

You do not want to continue living a situation that you feel traps you and makes you unhappy, you may have to cut some ties definitively.

In the professional area, you can exploit your knowledge beyond the mental boundaries that you had set for yourself.

From an economic point of view, you will have to be more cautious with your transactions, as you could act without thinking and make mistakes that can lead to bankruptcy.

If you have a partner, it is time to talk honestly, explain that you want to regain your freedom. Your confession will be like a bombshell, but it is very meditated.

For those who do not have a partner, agreeing to look beyond the veil of illusion will help you discover that the person you had your eyes on cannot offer you true love.

Lucky Numbers

4, 5, 25, 28, 32

March 2025

This month some Geminis will decide to break up with their partner, something that is not an easy topic to digest from an emotional point of view. For some it will be like a liberation and for others a disappointment.

If you do not have a partner, you will decide not to waste time with people who do not give you what you aspire to.

In the professional area, a month of expansion awaits you, you must take advantage of the opportunities that present themselves to progress and go further.

Luck accompanies all those who have exams this month, take advantage of these energies.

Watch out for reckless spending between 5 and 17, as you might regret it.

You need to take care of yourself, look for what brings you peace, interesting projects will come, but now is the time to heal the wounds.

Despite the responsibilities, never neglect your dreams. Life is too short to be saturated with obligations. Only then will you be able to feel triumphant.

Your intellectual acuity will help you better understand the challenges that will arise and your ability to make decisions will contribute to your success in a project.

At the end of the month, you will feel ample satisfaction in watching your progress, which nothing can stop you from continuing to succeed.

Lucky Numbers

6, 8, 15, 22, 35

April 2025

This month remember that not everything that crosses your mind will be palpable in the material world. Remember that your prolific imagination can take you extremely far, and make you move away from reality.

On the sentimental level, you are in a contradictory state with respect to your partner and it is difficult for you to distinguish between truths and lies. You trust your partner, you know that he or she is the right person for you, but you have many doubts. Stop foreshadowing the worst or you will end up drawing it to you. Your imagination makes you see ghosts where there are none.

If you do not have a partner, someone will fan the flame of love in you, and you see yourself already living a love story with that person.

Your finances and your businesses will be quite stable, and at a professional level. Your dreams align with reality on a financial level. You could say that you make you envious, because you have the possibility of spending to buy everything you like.

Some may receive a good sum of money because of a legal process, the verdict is favorable to you, and you are likely to receive a considerable amount of money in damages. You imagined the worst; however, you get a big win.

Those who are dedicated to sales businesses have an excellent end of the month. The money you get is invested.

Some muscle pain will alert you that something may be complicating your health, it is not serious, but you should see a doctor.

Lucky Numbers

4, 13, 20, ,28, 30

May 2025

This month you will probably oscillate between extreme joy and abysses of anxiety, especially on a sentimental level.

You can organize your life because there are a planetary aspect that will push you down and bring you down from the clouds.

This month you must seek the balance between unbridled optimism and pessimism. You give too much power to your mind; this leads you down paths where you risk losing control of your life. If you do not have a clear and objective view, you may have to make sudden decisions that will affect your bank account.

You can start a particularly good business but beware of your tendency to overestimate your capabilities. The planets advise you to be cautious so that you do not fall into the nets of unscrupulous people.

Those who do not have a partner will be in luck since the person they are interested in after the 19th finally responds to their messages.

It will be a month in which you will have many things to think about, you must avoid distractions and waste of time. Focus your energies on your business. You will be able to pay off all your debts, but this will require you to put aside your disorganization. Tranquility and economic balance will return to your life.

At the end of the month you will develop projects that are important to you and that could be very lucrative. Take the opportunity to try your luck at gambling.

Between the 25th and the 30th, the planets will favor communication regarding a friendship with romantic overtones.

Lucky Numbers

6, 10, 19, 24, 30

June 2025

This month you have a great deal of luck, and you will be able to spot malicious and envious people from miles away.

Bring your dreams to life, you will be presented with career opportunities to achieve what you want. The planets will provide you with enough energy to start your own business. Take the opportunity to lay the foundations for your future.

In love, you get away from arguments and acquire a pleasant mode of communication. What you really want is to have a healthy relationship with your partner and humor is your tool to enjoy the month.

If your heart still has no owner, you will finally receive pleasant news. If you have someone in mind for a long time, things will be unlocked, and you could live a real romance with that person.

After the 20th is the ideal time to review your personal projects, as you have creative ideas and solutions.

Start with small steps, and you will get the momentum you need to implement the changes you want. Do not tell everyone about your plans, some people out of envy may sabotage you, instead of support. ng you.

Your projects are treasures that you must protect discreetly. When they are strong enough you can expose them without fear.

Lucky Numbers

10,19,27,28,29

July 2025

A month where you will enjoy the affection of your partner, and it will be reciprocal. A new joint project could strengthen your bond. If you do not have a partner, it is a good time to talk to new people and get in touch.

At work, you will find solutions and enjoy a peaceful and pleasant working life. Your intellectual acuity will help you find the information you need to excel in your work.

On an economic level you can relax since luck will accompany you in all the businesses you want to do. Your steps move quickly towards success, and your ability to adapt is a real tool in your life.

Do not look back, you can build an empire from scratch. Victory and success are your destiny, thanks to your perseverance.

In the middle of the month, a planetary aspect drives you to make healthy changes in your relationship. Your behavior is a key factor in the problems you currently have. Solves all problems at the root. You may not like what you discover, but you can start over on a healthy footing with your significant other.

Winds of change are announced at the end of the month for those who do not have a partner. Someone from the past is about to make an appearance again, you should weigh the pros and cons before deciding whether to give that person a second chance.

Lucky Numbers
17, 22, 26, 31, 36

August 2025

This month favors matters of the heart for those who do not have a partner. You may not have any desire to revisit an old story, but heaven sends you signs of a reconciliation with someone you adored in the past.

There is still some chemistry between the two of you, and you need to decide whether to give that person a second chance.

After the 6th, some will sacrifice the security of a permanent job to start a business of their own. Do not be afraid of obstacles, or challenges. You must trust in your potential to achieve success.

This month you attract good fortune like a magnet and your bank account will always be positive, you do not run the risk of losses.

Geminis will enjoy exceptional material prosperity. Money calls money, which is why you will get good news after the 21st. Maybe you get a refund, a bonus, or get a ticket in the lottery.

You are living a phase of abundance this month and you will be able to make all situations tilt in your favor. This good streak should not make you forget that you have flaws and that you need to work on your dark areas.

At the end of the month, try to give your professional image a break.

Avoid divulging the details of your love life to your colleagues, stay away from gossip.

Lucky Numbers

6 – 10 – 19 – 24 - 30

September 2025

This month, if you have been working on a creative project, your efforts will be rewarded. It is wise to stick with your positive thoughts so that even more interesting ideas can flourish in your mind.

Make sure you are gentle in your dealings with others, as success does not give you the right to be an inconsiderate person to those around you.

Those who do not have a partner are not willing to be influenced by family and traditions. You will be aware of what is preventing you from finding the right partner. If you keep your parents' criteria in mind, you will never find the person who really suits you.

Those who are in a relationship will prioritize love and ignore disagreements and will be more willing to forgive unimportant things. You will be willing to start over with your better half and distance yourself from the daily grind.

After the 21st, some may receive unpleasant news related to work. Do not panic because this is a unique opportunity to start a new cycle in your life. Without a doubt, it is the opportunity to assert your skills and not depend on anyone else.

The last days of the month you will be overly excited about a particularly good idea, but you must move calmly and not lose focus.

This month you should start giving your body movement, start eating healthier and leave junk food aside.

Lucky Numbers
7, 11, 13, 16, 26

October 2025

During the month of October you will have the opportunity to change jobs. You will also be presented with several investment opportunities. However, take the time to analyze them before putting your economy at risk.

It is important that you have faith in your destiny so that it will guide you to the right place. This month you will grow in every sense of the word; you will regain your personal power and vindicate your convictions. You are willing to improve your life.

It is important that you do not resist the transformation, but that you let yourself go, as it will undoubtedly lead you to better situations for you. You must modify your thinking pattern. If you embrace change, new opportunities will broaden your horizons beyond your expectations.

This month your heart is cold because you gave a lot and received little in return, it will be good for you to heal.

After the 15th you will fight not to fall into episodes of sadness and anxiety, learn to listen to advice. You should do exercises to calm what you feel.

If you are in a relationship, or engaged, a piece of news from someone from your past is going to shake up the relationship. A problematic person will show signs of life and have contact with you. It is best to stay away to avoid conflict with your partner.

At the end of the month you can plan to invest in your house. If you already have one, you can remodel or redecorate it. This is a good month to improve your own space.

Lucky Numbers
13 16 28 31 33

November 2025

This month if you do not have a partner, the Moon will help you find a person who will make you happy. You have the protection of higher forces; you will come out of loneliness and sadness. You are convinced that you will find the person with whom you can build lasting happiness.

After the 5th begins to heal your emotional wounds, a better future awaits you. When you stop waiting for love, that is when it arrives without warning. You must go out and try your luck.

Before starting a long-term project, you should take the time to choose the best option. In fact, take a step back to analyze the situation and be able to make the most effective decision. In the professional area you have all doors open. You may receive unexpected information indicating potential sources of income. Whatever it is, new opportunities are going to present themselves that could make a big difference in your lifestyle.

Things could get serious after the 11th, and this could be the energy you need to take a relationship to the next level.

At the end of the month, if you feel bored, it is vital that you look for new challenges so you can avoid that feeling of being unfocused.

It is time for you to try new things, accept that what happened had to be that way. Stop locking yourself in your thoughts, give life a chance to surprise you.

Lucky Numbers

15 21 23 31 36

December 2025

Last month of the year, if you do not have a partner, you must get out of your comfort zone, fear is preventing you from living life to the fullest. Avoid falling into self-criticism, do not torture yourself with questions about what you did wrong or what you failed at.

Luck will allow you to keep your head on your shoulders, choose your wars and know where it can be profitable for you to invest your money and energy. You must recharge your batteries for next year. Do not wear yourself out with stupid situations. Stop trying to solve the lives of others. If the rest do not know what they want to do with their life, that is not your problem.

In the middle of the month you should keep your manners because you run the risk of upsetting your partner, who may not feel emotionally the same as you.

If you do not have a partner, accept opening yourself up to life like a flower in the sun's rays. It is time for you to allow yourself to live freely so that you can meet lovely people. A beautiful love story can arise, but for that you must get rid of your fears. If you manage to overcome that self-blocking, you will be able to spread your wings and seduce whoever you want.

At the end of the month, someone in your family will want to tell you what you should do with your money, without you having asked for advice. Do not respond with sarcasm, be kind.

You should calm your desires to spend money on sumptuous gifts, think carefully before spending your money.

It is the end of the year, so try to free yourself from things that bind you, from people who do not do you good, and stress you out.

Try to rest as much as you can, disconnect, and forget about the world is key to starting a year 2026 with your feet on the ground.

Lucky Numbers
11, 12, 22 30, 31

The Tarot Cards, an Enigmatic and Psychological World.

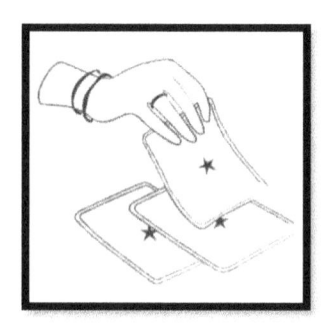

The word Tarot means "royal road", it is an ancient practice, it is not known exactly who invented card games in general, nor the Tarot in particular; There are the most dissimilar hypotheses in this regard. Some say that it arose in Atlantis or Egypt, but others believe that tarots came from China or India, from the ancient land of the Gypsies, or that they came to Europe through the Cathars.

The fact is that tarot cards distill astrological, alchemical, esoteric, and religious symbolisms, both Christian and pagan.

Until recently some people if you mentioned the word 'tarot' it was common for them to imagine a gypsy sitting in front of a crystal ball in a room surrounded by mysticism, or to think of black magic or witchcraft, today this has changed.

This ancient technique has been adapting to the new times, it has joined technology, and many young people feel a deep interest in it.

Young people have isolated themselves from religion because they consider that they will not find the solution to what they need, they realized the duality of religion, something that does not happen with spirituality.

On all social networks you find accounts dedicated to the study and readings of the tarot, since everything related to esotericism is fashionable, in fact, some hierarchical decisions are made taking into account tarot or astrology.

The remarkable thing is that the predictions that are usually related to the tarot are not the most sought-after, what is related to self-knowledge and spiritual advice is the most requested.

The tarot is an oracle, through its drawings and colors, we stimulate our psychic sphere, the most recondite part that goes beyond the natural. Several people turn to the tarot as a spiritual or psychological guide, since we live in times of uncertainty, and this pushes us to look for answers in spirituality.

It is such a powerful tool that it tells you concretely what is going on in your subconscious so that you can perceive it through the lenses of a new wisdom.

Carl Gustav Jung, the famous psychologist, used the symbols of tarot cards in his psychological studies. He created the theory of archetypes, where he discovered an extensive sum of images that help in analytical psychology.

The use of drawings and symbols to appeal to a deeper understanding is frequently used in psychoanalysis. These allegories are part of us, corresponding to symbols of our subconscious and our mind.

Our unconscious has dark areas, and when we use visual techniques, we can reach different parts of it and reveal elements of our personality that we do not know.

When you manage to decode these messages through the pictorial language of the tarot, you can choose what decisions to make in life to create the destiny you really want.

The tarot with its symbols teaches us that there is a different Universe, especially today where everything is so chaotic, and a logical explanation is sought for all things.

The Star, Tarot Card for Gemini 2025

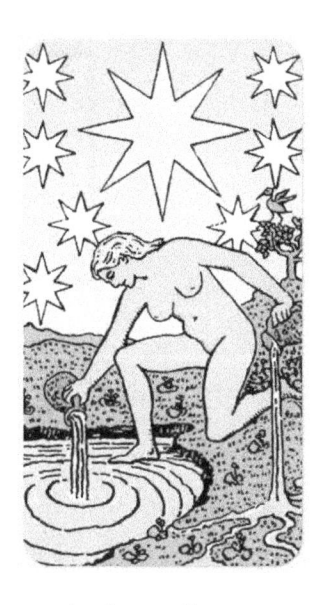

The Star symbolizes optimism. In case of conflicts, he reminds you that there is always hope, you must never lose faith. Indicate that you are going to receive surprise help. The Star guides you, accompanies you along the way, and provides clarity, helping you to perceive a larger truth. The Star helps you develop your intuition and connects you to ancient knowledge.

The Star will give you calm, tranquility, serenity, and rest. The Star refers to an intense and passionate love, which is also going to be an important relationship for you. If you want to get pregnant, this card announces a pregnancy. Likewise, the energy of this card favors long-term projects.

Lucky Colors

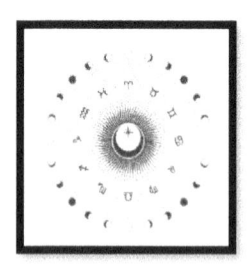

Colors affect us psychologically; They influence our appreciation of things, opinion about something or someone, and can be used to influence our decisions.

The traditions to welcome the new year vary from country to country, and on the night of December 31 we balance all the positive and negative that we experienced in the year that is leaving. We begin to think about what to do to transform our luck in the new year that is approaching.

There are several ways to attract positive energies to us when we receive the new year, and one of them is to wear or wear accessories of a specific color that attracts what we want for the year that is about to begin.

Colors have energetic charges that influence our lives, so it is always advisable to receive the year dressed in a color that attracts the energies of what we want to achieve.

For that there are colors that vibrate positively with each zodiac sign, so the recommendation is that you wear clothes with the shade that will attract prosperity, health, and love in 2025. (You can also wear these colors throughout the rest of the year for important occasions, or to enhance your days.)

Remember that, although the most common is to wear red underwear for passion, pink for love and yellow or gold for abundance, it never hurts to attach to our outfit the color that most benefits our zodiac sign.

Gemini

Orange

A color that is in nature, in fruits and in glamorous sunsets.

Orange is a color that gives off warmth.

It is a color that invokes enthusiasm, passion, and confidence. It is related to happiness, creativity, and vitality.

Orange is a particularly good color for situations where there may be problems with shyness. It will help you overcome obstacles and challenges as it will instill courage and determination in you.

This color will help you create new bonds. This shade repels negative energies, and helps you stand out from the rest.

The vibrant and striking presence of this color will give you confidence to express your emotions and ideas.

Lucky Charms

Who does not own a lucky ring, a chain that you never take off, or an object you would not give away for anything in this world? We all attribute a special power to certain items that belong to us and that special character they assume for us makes them magical objects. For a talisman to act and influence circumstances, its bearer must have faith in it, and this will transform it into a prodigious object, capable of fulfilling everything that is asked of it.

In the everyday sense, an amulet is any object that promotes good as a preventive measure against evil, harm, disease, and witchcraft.

 Good luck charms can help you have a year 2025 full of blessings in your home, work, with your family, attract money and health. For the amulets to work properly, you should not lend them to anyone else, and you should always have them on hand.

Amulets have existed in all cultures, and they are made from elements of nature that serve as catalysts for energies that help create human desires.

The amulet is assigned the power to ward off evils, spells, diseases, disasters, or counteract evil desires cast through other people's eyes.

Gemini

Tree of Life.

The tree of life symbolizes the connection of all things in the world. The circle symbolizes the world, and the roots and branches represent everything within it.

This amulet will help you have wisdom, strength, and knowledge as it has a unique connection to ancestral roots and life after death.

This charm will protect you, give you inspiration, help you focus, and remind you that we are all part of a larger universal whole.

This amulet symbolizes longevity, it will make you more confident and stronger. It symbolizes togetherness and serves as a reminder that you are never alone or isolated but connected to the world. This tree of life charm is found in many cultures and can protect you and help you get through any difficult situation.

Its energy is compatible with both men, and will always help you maintain peace, and tranquility, in your home and protect you from the forces of evil. It is an immensely powerful amulet for a pregnant woman, symbolizing the beginning of a new life. He will protect the child and the mother from evil and give him wisdom.

Lucky Quartz for 2025

We are all attracted to diamonds, rubies, emeralds, and sapphires, they are obviously precious stones. Semi-precious stones such as carnelian, tiger's eye, white quartz, and lapis lazuli are also highly prized as they have been used as ornaments and symbols of power for thousands of years.

What many do not know is that they were valued for more than just their beauty: each one had a sacred meaning, and its healing properties were as important as its ornamental value.

Crystals still have the same properties today, most people are familiar with the most popular ones such as amethyst, malachite and obsidian, but currently there are new crystals such as larimar, petalite and phenacite that have become known.

A crystal is a solid body with a geometrically regular shape, crystals were formed when the earth was created and have continued to metamorphose as the planet has been changing, crystals are the DNA of the earth, they are miniature warehouses that contain the development of our planet over millions of years.

Some have been brought under extraordinary pressures and others grew in chambers buried deep underground, others dripped into being. Whatever shape they take, their crystalline structure can absorb, preserve, focus, and emit energy.

At the heart of the crystal is the atom, its electrons, and protons. The atom is dynamic and is composed of a series of particles that rotate around the center in constant motion, so that although the crystal may appear motionless, it is a living molecular mass vibrating at a certain frequency, and this is what gives the crystal its energy.

Gems used to be a royal and priestly prerogative, the priests of Judaism wore a plaque on their chest full of precious stones which was much more than an emblem to designate their function, since it transferred power to those who wore it.

Men have used stones since the Stone Age as they had a protective function by guarding their wearers from various evils. Today's crystals have the same power, and we can select our jewelry not only based on their external attractiveness, having them close to us can enhance our energy (orange carnelian), cleanse the space around us (amber) or attract wealth (citrine).

Certain crystals such as smoky quartz and black tourmaline can absorb negativity, emitting pure and clean energy.

Wearing a black tourmaline around your neck protects you from electromagnetic fumes including that of cell phones, a citrine will not only attract riches, but also help you preserve them, place it in the wealth part of your home (the back left furthest from the front door).

If you are looking for love, crystals can help you, place a rose quartz in the corner of relationships in your house (the back right corner furthest from the front door) its effect is so powerful that it is advisable to add an amethyst to compensate for the attraction.

You can also use rhodochrosite, love will come your way.

Crystals can heal and give balance, some crystals contain minerals known for their therapeutic properties, malachite has a high concentration of copper, wearing a malachite bracelet allows the body to absorb minimal amounts of copper.

Lapis lazuli relieves migraine, but if the headache is caused by stress, amethyst, amber, or turquoise placed on the eyebrows will relieve it.

Quartz and minerals are jewels of mother earth, give yourself the chance, and connect with the magic they give off.

Lucky Quartz Gemini /2025

Tourmaline' Black.

It acts as a powerful energy absorber as a psychic void to release and remove all density, and darkness from your energy field, and your entire being. It is a great stone to keep in your pocket when you are in an area full of people, especially if you tend to absorb the emotions of others very easily.

Black tourmaline can act as a defensive shield against any harmful energy and any mental and emotional manipulation. It keeps you focused on what is real.

This stone eliminates distractions, helping you move towards your goals. As you work with black tourmaline, you will notice that you are moving forward and progressing toward your goals, finding more clarity to structure your days.

You can use it to help you realize your dreams, ideas, and intentions through practical daily actions. It helps you stay rational, down-to-earth, disciplined, and patient to get what you want, and it will help you see the big picture of the road, heading straight to where you want to go.

It helps you stay grounded and realistic; while also clearing the fog so you can focus on the higher, more aligned goals that will help you serve your soul's purpose.

Compatibility of Gemini and the Zodiac Signs

Gemini is an air sign that can get along without problems among their friends, parties, and nights of rumba. Gemini is ruled by Mercury, the planet of communication, so you can always find interesting topics to talk about

Gemini is an excellent anecdotist, and their dynamic energy and magnetism attract romantic partners. Jealous people should know that Gemini is never alone, as they always have fans and followers. As Gemini expresses their emotions externally, they love to converse. This self-expression is paramount for the mercurial twin, so he needs all lines of communication to be open, and willing to receive information, to his Geminian.

He does not care how his ideas are conveyed, the action of sharing his thoughts is more important than what he says. There is nothing Gemini despises more than leisure; he is always busy. He does not stop making dealings with his multiple entertainments, inclinations, and social obligations.
This air sign may complain about being overworked, but when you analyze their daily schedule all their errands are optional, which shows that Gemini's schedule is nothing more than the result of their exclusive duality. Gemini loves to share their thoughts and ideas, but they do not know how to listen, they are easily distracted, so it is key that you make sure your Gemini partner pays attention to you.

If by chance you see that he moves away from the conversation, do not hesitate to tell him and remind him that communication is between two people. It is not easy to keep Gemini's interest, in fact, he does not know how to stay focused. This sign has pretty much seen it all and the best way to keep their gaze fixed is to keep it on their feet.

Make the necessary changes, and do not forget that you should never compromise your values or needs. As you get to know Gemini, have fun discovering your own multi-diversity. The seduction technique that works with Gemini is talking, and being the most multifaceted sign, they will love to tell you their hobbies and interests.

As it is so curious, conversing with this sign is like looking in the mirror, since it has the wonderful ability to reflect what you say to it. This may seem strange, but it really is the nature of this sign. Dating a Gemini is a stimulating experience, you must be careful because Gemini requires constant stimulation, which sometimes makes it difficult to get to know them on an emotional level deeply. Make sure you make time to sit down and chat with your fellow Gemini without distractions, and do not be afraid to remind them that pleasurable receptions are never wasted time.

Gemini loves sex, for him it is another form of communication. Gemini has a strong sexual appetite, and to turn him on, a couple of insightful comments are enough. When it comes to dirty talk, Gemini wrote an encyclopedia, so you can turn him on by explaining exactly what you like to do in bed. In this way he will feel and analyze at the same time, a combination that he is orgasmic.

One of the particularities of Gemini is how quickly it can recover from the most devastating mistakes. Unlike other signs, he is not governed by his ego. He likes to have fun, so he does not let his ego get in his way, so when he makes a mistake, he never gets defensive.

If Gemini has to offer an apology, they will do so immediately. Although this quality is super respected, it is not completely generous. Gemini expects you to accept their apology with the same haste.

Gemini is happiest when he is busy, as soon as his calendar gets too relaxed, he finds a way to change things up. It is not that he is scared, it is just that he does not like to be bored.

All of this can be challenging for Gemini couples. Stable relationships require a lot of care, and Gemini cannot offer it easily, so when you are in a relationship, you need to make sure you are prioritizing your relationships.

As this air sign is willing to try everything at least once, but sometimes twice, they enjoy exploring various aspects of their personality through their romantic relationships.

Although they do not project it, Gemini is looking for a serene partner who balances their intimate or family space, since for modifications they already have enough with theirs. This air sign is constantly looking for who they can maintain a good relationship with, and for that reason they are always rambling.

Gemini and Aries is a strong relationship with all kinds of dynamics including friendship, and romance. The same Aries, as Gemini, enjoy their mistakes and appreciate the impetus of the other. With their jokes, code words, and fun, Gemini and Aries bring out the best in each other.
The danger, however, is that neither Gemini nor Aries are particularly good at ending the night.
In this couple, it is important that someone takes responsibility. Otherwise, it can be difficult for these partygoers to cultivate a healthy and emotionally strong relationship.

Gemini and Taurus is not a comfortable relationship, but if you are both committed, you can achieve a long-lasting relationship. Taurus, with its strong character, is never afraid to set boundaries. Gemini has a completely different way of seeing the world, so he does not understand Taurus' avid demand for security. However, if they can negotiate between permanence and transience, they can educate each other invaluable lessons.

If Taurus and Gemini are willing to make substantial changes to compensate for each other's needs, this relationship has the potential to be challenging and entertaining.

Two Geminis, it is like a party in broad daylight. They understand each other deeply, and they never get tired. The problem with this couple is that they may lack perspective.
For a Gemini² relationship to be successful in the long run, each of you must make sure you learn to listen. Both of you will have a lot of innovative ideas, but unless one of you is willing to offer stability, you risk losing control and killing the relationship.

Gemini and Cancer can build a beautiful relationship if they wish. Cancer has a very characteristic approach to life because it is overly sensitive and intuitive, and needs a lot of love, and validation to feel safe.
At first, it may seem like the cerebral Gemini could never offer that kind of setup, but Gemini is flexible. If Cancer knows how to communicate their needs directly, Gemini will strive to meet their requirements.

Cancer's deep emotions and sensitivity are also challenged by Gemini's detachment. However, if Gemini takes off the mask, this may be a couple worth keeping.

Ultimately, while this relationship requires a bit of effort and investment, these signs can build a compassionate and fun connection.

Gemini and Leo are the spirit of any party, together they form an effective and active couple that must be noticed and listened to. Leo is seduced by being the center of the action and there is nothing that seduces Gemini more than finding celebration.

These two social ambassadors are happy in meetings, but they differ on many points.
Leo loves to shine in front of the public, but in the end what he is looking for is an honest relationship.

Gemini, on the other hand, is not interested in impressing anyone. In fact, Gemini cares about feeding their eager cravings for curiosity. When Leo wants to establish trust, Gemini wants to have fun.
As a result, Leo may view Gemini as insensitive, while Gemini may be frustrated by Leo's needs.
However, through communication, they can learn to have a relationship based on search and fun.

Gemini and Virgo are ruled by Mercury, the planet of communication, so they share a sublime understanding and appreciation for expression. However, despite this influence, these two signs have quite different ways of transmitting information. Gemini is all elusive, while Virgo is eminently accessible.

Gemini is insightful and quick with their thoughts, while Virgo, an astute analyst and processor, prefers ideas only after organizing them properly. As a result, a relationship between these two signs requires them to work hard to ensure that they share and listen to each other equally.

Otherwise, Gemini is likely to end up monopolizing the conversation, while Virgo stores up a taciturn anger toward their exorbitantly chatty comrade.

Gemini is sociable and can also make Virgo frantic or jealous, however, when each sign lets their guard down and decides to have fun, this relationship has potential.

Between **Gemini and** Libra there is an instant connection when they mate. Both are aligned in full balance. The two of them share fun talks, charming stories, and many fabulous festivities. However, tightness can arise when Libra, with all its glamour, is let down by Gemini's jokes.

The truth is that Gemini talks about everything with anyone, and Libra is more selective when it comes to starting a conversation, something that Gemini can find a bit presumptuous. However, if each sign can comply with the other's approach, the couple can last a long time.

Gemini and Scorpio are easily uneven. Gemini is too busy with life's many emotions to get caught up in a specific drama, while Scorpio would never dare let his guard down unless he knew it was a reality.

Interestingly, Gemini and Scorpio are attracted to each other in a powerful and seductive way. Gemini is hypnotized by Scorpio's spirituality, and Scorpio is preoccupied with trying to win Gemini's affection.

At first, the relationship is stimulated by desire, but once the couple is instituted, they must face some significant difficulties. The resourceful Gemini needs freedom, while the mighty Scorpio demands unwavering loyalty.

And while Gemini is flexible, Scorpio holds on to their feelings, so it is important for both of you to practice reading each other's ways. This couple is not easy, but they have extraordinary chemistry, especially sexual, and this can make this relationship worth all the work.

Gemini and Sagittarius are compatible, in fact, this couple is one of the most dynamic in the entire zodiac. These signs are naturally wanderers, and when they come together, they form an incredibly exquisite power couple who love recreation.

They have like-minded approaches to life and approach the world with the same frenzy, and optimism. Gemini and Sagittarius are natural storytellers, and the mental stimulation between these two signs causes neurons to project at high speed.

Basically, it is a relationship that does not require much work, but they should not take their relationship for granted. Every relationship requires trust and commitment, so you both need to make sure you do not take too many liberties.

Circumstantially, the ego of Sagittarius can cause problems, but Gemini with its suggestion skills will know how to channel the circumstances. Obviously, Sagittarius has a lot to boast about, but they should be humbler.

Gemini and Capricorn is a relationship that takes a lot of dedication. Capricorn is enthralled by Gemini. The hardest working sign of the zodiac does not understand how someone so erratic can achieve so many successes. While Capricorn wears himself out working, Gemini, like a sorcerer shows the varied ways in which he achieves success, leaving Capricorn in awe and completely in love.

Through communication, these two can gradually learn to understand each other better. To build a healthy relationship, Capricorn must consent to Gemini changing their mind frequently.

Gemini must communicate his thought process to Capricorn, so that his earthly companion can reason out the reasons for his disproportionate changes of mind. In short, the dynamics of this relationship can work, but it will require dedication on both sides.

Gemini and Aquarius have similar ideas. Aquarius is very intrigued by the insightful Gemini, and Gemini is enchanted by Aquarius' unalterable attitude and deeply humanitarian passion.

Gemini and Aquarius understand each other maturely and know how to sharpen each other's imaginations with great dialogue. However, Aquarius is known for his rebellious extremist ideas, which, while wonderful, can annoy Gemini, who often prefers familiarity to rebellion. However, despite a small ellipse of instruction, it is easy for these two to learn to be together. This relationship can develop into a formal and lasting romance over time.

Gemini and Pisces have a complex relationship. As Gemini is personified by twins, this air sign carries its duality on the face. On the other hand, the multiple profiles of Pisces are less visible to the naked eye.
The sign of Pisces represents two united fish that move in opposite directions, symbolizing their relationship with both the subtle and earthly realms.
As both have two faces, they understand each other's need for freedom and investigation. However, neither Gemini nor Pisces are good at creating limits, so this couple must fight hard to create a dynamic.
Pisces is sensitive and can be suspicious of the purposes behind Gemini's cunning subtlety. Meanwhile, Gemini is likely to think that Pisces is overly dramatic. To function, this couple needs to communicate honestly and without games.

Gemini and Vocation

Gemini has excellent mental agility and is very curious. It is a sign that knows how to take advantage of opportunities to increase their knowledge.

Her communication skills, and mastery of multiple topics, are synchronized to allow her to relate easily in the areas she frequents.

Monotony does not fit with this sign. They have a need for intellectual stimulation and to persistently expand their knowledge, in various areas of interest. Gemini's impatient nature requires constant changes. Otherwise, their spirit is discouraged and destroyed.

Best Professions

Geminis are multifaceted people. It is the most affable, friendly, and communicative sign of the zodiac. They are best suited to careers that interact with the public and offer variety. They are very versatile, which is why they are prone to change professions many times. Journalism, media in general, musical, or theatrical performers, public relations, writers, and sales.

Stress. An obstacle on the road to 2025

We often try so hard to achieve our goals that we end up stressed and frustrated that we do not get the results we want.

Avoid having stress because that state is a trap that prevents prosperity from coming into your life. If you are stressed, it means that you live in a state of lack.

You may have financial pressure, but maintaining a calm inner state is a decisive element in achieving your goal of prosperity. When you are relaxed, and anxiety-free, all the good things start to happen because you are in tune with your aspirations, rather than feeling the lack of what you are aiming for.

Stress will not benefit you at all. Wanting something so intensely that it causes you stress is not worth it. Flowing with the Universe, being in the here and now, and enjoying the moment, are crucial to getting everything you want.

Focus on the future and repeat positive affirmations so that you can increase your self-confidence and reprogram your mind. Learn to be content with what you have right now.

We have all felt stress when we have been faced with extreme demands, or sudden changes. But some individuals are so addicted to stress, they have it as a lifestyle.

Do not dream for a minute of your life that none of us are going to have a stress-free life, for that you would have to choose another planet (and I have not been consciously on any, so I cannot give you recommendations).

Stress is not always harmful. One aspect that divides harmless stress from harmful stress that makes you sick is the duration of time.

We all can deal with temporary periods of stress, if they are not excessively painful, and exhausting. The problem arises when we remain stressed for long periods of time since the human body is not designed for this.

Unfortunately, every day our environment becomes more stressful, and we look like butterflies trapped in the spider webs of stress. But not all of us experience stress in the same way because, although external causes are out of our control, it takes more than these for stress to harm us.

The challenges that life puts at us are not as important as our inner world. That is, the way we think, feel, and behave in response to these circumstances. Stress is an illusion formed by our minds to adjust our way of seeing the world.

Tell me how often that thing you fear so much happened?

We all feel fear, to a lesser or greater extent, most days of our lives of something chaotic happening in our lives.

You must remember on those days that the illusion of stress feeds on our pretensions to guess the future. We long for the obligation to foresee the future, to keep it in sight. That obsession, of having power and control, is what fuels stress.

On the other side of the coin are afraid of losing all the blessings and material things they have. I have news for all those people: if they are going to lose everything, even their own lives.
No one is born to seed and when you leave you do not take anything from this world. But in the meantime, enjoy this journey that has its ups and downs, accept the challenges and changes, do not anticipate, and do not have stress.

There is a gift hidden within stress. Underneath all that anxiety, you have a strong personality waiting for you to open the door for him. The key is yours alone.

People who live peacefully achieve prosperity faster.

Digital Narcissism

Narcissism, a personality disorder with multiple and complicated causes, has become a profoundly serious problem. Living in a cruelly selfish system, with an avid obsession with acquiring economic power, and in a society that popularizes aggressive competition in all spheres of life, narcissistic behaviors have worsened.

Social networks have become the perfect terrain for all kinds of narcissistic behaviors. The possibility of fabricating an enhanced, embellished, and enhanced image, to obtain admirers and approval through "likes" or followers, attracts people with this personality disorder.

A narcissist is a person who requires exaggerated admiration, has an irrational aura of superiority, and uses others to his advantage. They are vain and arrogant people.

How can you spot them? If you take a walk-through Instagram or Facebook, you will notice the number of people who consistently live for the permanent exhibition of their physique through provocative images.

They do this to counteract their inferiority complex, and lack of self-esteem. There are others who try to communicate a perfect life above the real odds, or establish emotional ties to receive praise, and then publicly offend and denigrate anyone who tries to contradict them.

Some seek compassion by publicly exaggerating any difficulty or misfortune they suffer to win the consideration and support of their followers, and there are those who hope to obtain praise and congratulations after public statements where they lower themselves and present themselves as someone humble, when behind that presumptuous modesty and excessive simplicity what is actually hidden is an extreme pride that needs to be reaffirmed on a recurring basis.

The disinhibiting and empathetic effect that digital media facilitates helps the narcissistic propagation. On social networks they have their path clear to project everything they would like to be and are not. These behaviors are typical of individuals who are emotionally lacking in affection.

We must protect our children, instilling in them the conscious and responsible use of networks, and educate them to accept themselves with their virtues and defects.

Adults who reject their own lives and characterize a figure they are not really by seeking continuous social approval must seek a healthy balance between the virtual world and reality.

Avoid comparing yourself with others, remember that networks only expose a tiny part of life, do not feed the desire for validation.

It is not necessary to close social networks, but to implement certain limits to their use because, although it may seem good and entertaining, the habit of seeing "likes" on social networks engenders addiction, anguish and overwhelm.

Narcissism is not linked to the totality of the time spent on social networks; narcissism is connected to the reasons why social networks are compulsively resorted to.

There is so much lavish presumptuousness, so many people who need to be the center of the Universe, even if they must take part in inappropriate, embarrassing, or abnormal behavior, which cause concern.

This wave of digital narcissism has real-world implications. One of the most disturbing is that individuals with narcissistic traits are more likely to be interested in politics.

As social networks amplify these effects, those who dominate public discourse and media debates are favored, with the number of "likes" being considered a reliable indicator of the level of knowledge and potential of that person.

There are currently narcissists on social media who promote hatred of people who think incorrectly or differently, this is destructive to social change because they do not build alliances, they only promote divisions.

We need more education about this phenomenon to reduce the harmful effects it has on a psychological level, both on those who suffer from the disorder and its victims, social media has increased cases of narcissism by creating an environment in which the number of likes and followers is a measure of success and popularity.

The Moon in Gemini

The Moon is not comfortable in the sign of Gemini. Air signs do not know how to deal with intense emotions, and Gemini specifically moves so fast that maintaining deep emotions is exceedingly difficult for them.

The Moon in Gemini is usually expressed with small flashes accompanied by sudden mood swings.

Gemini prefers to act in the social and mental area.

The Moon in Gemini wants to be free to explore duality and experience the full range of emotions, moving freely between opposite ends of a situation.

If your Moon is in the sign of Gemini, you will feel more confident when you explore novel ideas and enjoy interacting socially with others.

Gemini is a sign that works best by operating on the surface as it is not interested in delving into the emotional world.

If your Moon is in Gemini, your comfort zone is related to keeping a range of options open. You need to feel that you are free to create your own opinion about different situations. You are always going to feel more comfortable when you can focus on more abstract and intellectual matters.

Words and language are specifically more important to you. All your safety-related concerns involve how you communicate with yourself in any situation.

The importance of the Rising Sign

The sun sign has a major impact on who we are, but the ascendant is what really defines us, and even that could be the reason you do not identify with some traits of your zodiac sign.

Really the energy that your sun sign gives you makes you feel different from the rest of the people, for that reason, when you read your horoscope sometimes you feel identified and it makes sense of some predictions, and that happens because it helps you understand how you could feel and what will happen to you, but it only shows you a percentage of what it could really be.

The ascendant on the other hand differs from the sun sign because it reflects who we are superficially, that is, how others see you or the energy you transmit to people, and this is so real that it may be the case that you meet someone and if you predict their sign it is possible that you have discovered their rising sign and not their sun sign.

In short, the characteristics you see in someone when you meet them for the first time is the ascendant, but because our lives are affected by the way we relate to others, the ascendant has an important impact on our daily lives.

It is a bit complex to explain how the ascendant sign is calculated or determined, because it is not the position of a planet that determines it, but the sign that rose on the eastern horizon at the time of your birth, unlike your sun sign, it depends on the precise time you were born.

Thanks to technology and the Universe today it is easier than ever to know this information, of course if you know your time of birth, or if you have an idea of the time but there is no margin of more hours, because there are many websites that make the calculation by entering the data, astro.com is one of them, but there are infinite ones.

In this way, when you read your horoscope you can also read your ascendant and know more personalized details, you will see that from now on if you do this your way of reading the horoscope will change and you will know why that Sagittarius is so modest and pessimistic if in reality they are so exaggerated and optimistic, and this is perhaps because they have a Capricorn Ascendant, or because that Scorpio colleague is always talking about everything, do not doubt that he has a Gemini Ascendant.

I am going to synthesize the characteristics of the different ascendants, but this is also very general since these characteristics are modified by planets in conjunction with the Ascendant, planets that aspect the

Ascendant, and the position of the ruling planet of the sign in the Ascendant.

For example, a person with an Aries Ascendant with its ruling planet, Mars, in Sagittarius will respond to the environment a little differently than another person, also with an Aries Ascendant, but whose Mars is in Scorpio.

Similarly, a person with a Pisces Ascendant who has Saturn conjunct it will "behave" differently than someone with a Pisces Ascendant who does not look like it.

All these factors modify the Ascendant, astrology is overly complex, and horoscopes are not read or made with tarot cards, because astrology is not only an art, but also a science.

It can be common to confuse these two practices, and this is because, although they are two different concepts, they have some points in common. One of these common points is based on their origin, and that is that both procedures have been known since ancient times.

They are also similar in the symbols they use, since both present ambiguous symbols that must be interpreted, so it requires specialized reading, and it is necessary to have training to know how to interpret these symbols.

There are thousands of differences, but one of the main ones is that while in tarot the symbols are perfectly understandable at first glance, as they are figurative cards, although you have to know how to interpret them well, in astrology we observe an abstract system which it is necessary to know beforehand to interpret them, and of course it must be said that, Although we can recognize the tarot cards, not just anyone can interpret them correctly.

Interpretation is also a difference between the two disciplines because while the tarot does not have an exact temporal reference, since the cards are placed in time only thanks to the questions that are asked in the corresponding spread, in astrology reference is made to a specific position of the planets in history, and the systems of interpretation used by both are diametrically opposed.

The birth chart is the basis of astrology, and the most important aspect to make the prediction. The birth chart must be perfectly prepared for the reading to be successful and to learn more about the person.

To prepare an astrological chart, it is necessary to know all the data about the birth of the person in question.

It is necessary that it be known exactly, from the exact time when she gave birth, to the place where she gave birth.

The position of the planets at the time of birth will reveal to the astrologer the points he needs to prepare the birth chart.

Astrology is not only about knowing your future, but also about knowing the important points of your existence, both present and past, to make better decisions to decide your future.

Astrology will help you to know yourself better, so that you can change the things that block you or enhance your qualities.

And if the birth chart is the basis of astrology, the tarot spread is fundamental in the latter discipline. Just like the one who makes the astrological chart, the psychic who makes the tarot spread, will be the key to the success of your reading, so the best thing to do is to ask for recommended tarot readers, and although surely he will not be able to answer you concretely to all the doubts you have in your life, a correct reading of the tarot spread, and the cards that come out in this spread will help guide you about the decisions you make in your life.

In summary, Astrology and tarot use symbology, but the overriding question is how all this symbology is interpreted.

Truly a person who master's both techniques will undoubtedly be a great help to the people who are going to ask him for advice.

Many astrologers combine both disciplines, and regular practice has taught me that both tend to flow very well, providing an enriching component in all prediction topics, but they are not the same and you cannot do a horoscope with tarot cards, nor can you do a tarot reading with an astrological chart.

Ascendant in Gemini

If you have an Ascendant in Gemini, you face life with curiosity about everything around you.

You have a lot of versatility, and for that reason you have no difficulty adapting to any situation.

Sometimes you lose your focus easily because you are interested in too many things at once, and sometimes you do not get to secure any.

The partner is especially important to you, if you have the Ascendant in Gemini, since you are afraid of getting lost in your mental ocean and you need someone to help you get out of that labyrinth.

You always try to show a cheerful, charismatic, and sociable personality. You have a charming charisma and that is why it is easy for you to win people over.

Sometimes you can have absurd attitudes, this is because you are interested in too many things at once and this can be reflected in your attitude towards the environment.

People with Ascendant in Gemini can think something and within hours think the opposite, but that instability is part of their charm.

Aries – Ascendant Gemini

These people are very expressive, the initiative of Aries is combined with the curiosity of Gemini. These individuals like to always be exchanging ideas.

In the sentimental area, it is extremely easy for them to establish intimacy with their partners, but sometimes they can destabilize their partner because they are very unstable.

At work they are innovative people with a lot of initiative. Their creativity and ease of adapting to everything is outstanding.

It is possible that they get carried away by charlatanism, being prone to superficiality.

Taurus – Ascendant Gemini

Taurus with Gemini Ascendant are sensitive people.

In the workplace, they have an intuition for business and opportunities, they know how to keep secrets and interact when appropriate.

In their romantic relationships they are pleasant people, they know how to handle difficult situations, but they value their space very much, and this is a basic requirement for their relationships to work.

This ascendant has a tendency to isolation, especially if they go through a difficult moment, such as a love breakup.

Gemini – Ascendant Gemini

Gemini with Ascendant Gemini is a person who has reinforced the characteristics of this sign. They are individuals with great mental agility, and with infinite curiosity.

They are master's in communication and assimilate any idea easily, winning most of the discussions where they participate. They always have many friendships and relationships.

In the workplace, they will do very well in a job related to communication. However, their instability can make it difficult for them to finish their projects.

In love relationships they are not serious people. They are seductive, but they do not have the constancy to maintain something formal.

Sometimes they talk without thinking, saying the first thing that crosses their mind, and this causes a lot of problems.

Cancer – Gemini Ascendant

Cancer with Ascendant in Gemini are communicative, imaginative, and creative people.

They fall in love easily, but they also soon become disillusioned. These types of people are charming, but self-centered, and capricious.

In the workplace, they are devoted to work, have many business skills, and are very persuasive.

Leo – Ascendant Gemini

Leo with Ascendant in Gemini are sociable. Gemini's versatility allows Leo to be more flexible. They love to travel, to get to know new places, cultures, and thoughts.

In the workplace, they reason very quickly and are persuasive, managing to skillfully expose all their ideas.

In their romantic relationships they are professionals in the art of seduction. They love to attract attention and be listened to. They are not very given to commitment, as they need freedom and experimentation with multiple partners.

Virgo – Ascendant Gemini

This combination of signs is usually reserved, and they greatly appreciate their privacy and solitude.

In the workplace they love challenges, they are quite unstable, something that also manifests itself when starting a relationship.

They are more inclined towards platonic love, that is, a relationship that does not involve a commitment. To win them over, you must appeal to their intellectual side.

These people worry excessively about their family stability.

Libra – Gemini Ascendant

Libra with Gemini Ascendant are very extroverted and youthful people. In the workplace, they value everything that has to do with creativity.

In their romantic relationships they like to share their life with someone they enjoy, they are very faithful and usually their relationships are lasting since they are always in communication with their partner.

Some are usually prone to create false expectations when starting a relationship, which causes them to have many breakups.

Scorpio – Gemini Ascendant

Rising Scorpio Gemini is one of the most extraordinary minds. These people can achieve everything they set out to do, as they know how and when to activate their potential.

In the workplace, they have leadership skills and stand out for their energy and efficiency. They are productive and this always pushes them to success.

In their romantic relationships they are very rational, it is exceedingly difficult to decipher what they are thinking since they are people who do not like to expose their feelings.

If they set their minds to it, they can be romantic, although they are impulsive and impatient.

Sometimes they are manipulative people, and they can abuse their authority.

Sagittarius– Ascendant Gemini

Sagittarius with Gemini Ascendant are outgoing and pleasant people. However, they can have an unstable personality, changing tastes quickly. They have a great sense of justice and carefully analyze any situation to always reach the most impartial verdict.

In the workplace, they are always successful in the field of communications and are mediators within their company.

They value their partner very much; however, they must provide them with intellectual stimulation and provide them with conversation since they are people who love to talk.

Some have too many relationships, and do not seriously establish themselves with any of them.

Capricorn – Ascendant Gemini

Capricorn with Gemini Ascendant are people who have great perception and a lot of responsibility.

In the workplace, they show a lot of interest in everything they do.

In love they succeed because they concentrate their efforts to conquer the other person. However, it is difficult for them to be attracted to someone.

Some of these people are ironic, which makes it difficult for them to relate.

Aquarius – Gemini Ascendant

Aquarius with Gemini Ascendant are idealistic and philosophical people. They are kind and enjoy their freedom very much.

In the professional area they are receptive in any activity and stand out for their originality.

On the sentimental level, it is easy for them to start any type of relationship. However, they will value friendship over love, and they cannot stand being confined to a relationship.

They are very eccentric, sometimes exposing themselves to dangers to reaffirm their freedom.

Pisces – Ascendant Gemini

Pisces with Gemini Ascendant seeks professional fulfillment.

In the workplace, they show an incredible capacity for everything, even synchronously.

In love, due to their instability, they are difficult people to live with. This is a long-term difficulty. They are very susceptible to words.

Energy Cords

In life we are exposed to different types of energy cords that pollute us and interfere with our way of thinking and acting. Energy cords are energetic ties that we have with other people, cities, things, opinions, or past lives, and links that other people have with you.

Sometimes some of these energy cords come from past lives, or the time in between those lives.

These energy cords can affect us in a positive or negative way, which depends on the quality of those relationships. When a relationship between two members, or elements, is positive, the energetic exchange that takes place is beneficial. In the energetic cords of toxic relationships, the energy that is being exchanged is very harmful, so they affect our energetic vibration in a negative way.

From the perspective of the etheric field, these energy cords have the appearance of ties, through which each end of the parts is joined and favors this exchange of energies.

Sometimes those energy cords are so toxic that it is extremely difficult to break free or protect yourself from them. These types of energy cords are harmful bonds that we have cultivated over time and the care we dedicate to fostering relationships with other people, cities, houses, objects, creeds, dogmas, religions, and other lives.

The longer the relationship, the stronger the energy cord and the more difficult it is to break it.

There is a type of energetic cord that develops with people with whom we have had romantic relationships Specifically if the relationship was stable and for a long time, when the relationship ends those energetic cords are powerful and toxic.

These energy cords, which in the past were a source of transmission of emotions and positive feelings of love, become channels to transfer resentment towards the other person.

The energetic cord is more toxic and stressful if the rupture was dramatic, or there was betrayal. It does not matter if you do not communicate with that person, those types of energy cords remain active, and if you do not remove them, they can absorb, or contaminate, your energies.

When we have sex with another person, even if the encounter is brief and casual, we also create energetic cords. In all the contacts we have on an intimate or emotional level, we exchange energy. The energy cords may not be toxic, but you are still giving that person access to your energy field, and therefore they can steal your energy.

If the sexual encounter is against your will, as happens in sexual abuse, an energetic cord is created so strong that it makes it impossible for the victim to heal.

There is a wide diversity of relational energy cords that are harmful. The fundamental ones are the current ties with family members, ancestors, friends and acquaintances, partners and lovers, strangers, pets, places, beliefs, and past lives.

The energetic cords become toxic when the relationship is broken, specifically when there is codependency, manipulation, narcissism, control, and power plays.

At other times, the toxic energy cords are not related to people with whom we have a true friendship, but to people who appear to be friends and truly are envious and steal your good energies.

Those are the so-called friends who approach you with the aim of annoying you with their dramas, who never care about how you feel, who are always asking you for advice, and who require your attention, and support day and night. After interacting with them, you feel drained, and your spirits are on the floor.

Always before eliminating those types of energy cords you should honestly ask yourself the reasons why you allowed that type of person to enter your life.

Sometimes the energetic cords adhere to our aura when we pass strangers on the street, or when we connect with others through social networks, even though we have never had a physical relationship with those people.

However, the energy cords that form with strangers are weak and easier to break.

There are also **group energy cords** that unite two or more people who have shared experiences, such as friends, couples, or with classmates from school.

The dynamics of a group's energy cords reflect the quality of its relationships. In addition, each member of the group in turn has several energy cords that are deployed to other much smaller groups within the energy cord of the main group.

Commonly many group energy cords are composed of a main energy cord that has control over other individuals. An example would be when a group reports to a school leader, teacher, or principal.

The structure of the group energy cords is like a fabric with various bonds. The energetic sequences determine the type of relationships and the exchange of energy between its members.

The group energy cords can provide an extraordinary source of energy support, if the group dynamics are whole and healthy. If the group relationship is deteriorating, or when several members have tensions with each other, this can negatively affect the collective energy of the group's energy cord and induce a massive internal energy attack.

Along with the energy cords that are created between human beings, there is the possibility that we also have energy cords with animals that have been our pets. These relationships are just as strong as those established between humans, even stronger. Usually those relationships are not toxic, but if they caused us some physical harm, or we had an emotional dependence on those pets, the energy cord becomes toxic and affects our well-being.

We can also develop energy cordons with countries, capitals, and houses in which we have resided. These energetic cords can be positive or negative. The quality of the energy cord depends on the relationship we have had with those places.

No matter how far you are from a city, or a country, the energies of that place, and the negative events you experienced, will continue to affect you, unless you cut the negative energetic cords.

Often many people have karmic contracts that they have signed in past lives, and even covenants with spirits, which remain with them in this present life. These karmic contracts can be seen in the form of etheric bindings and knots at various points in your energy fields.

They are often contracts of poverty and suffering due to traumatic experiences. Regularly people who had clairvoyant abilities in other lifetimes, but suffered retaliation for it, tend to deny their intuitive abilities in this lifetime by creating an etheric knot in their third eye.

Usually, the reason why certain contracts, curses, or past life traumas persist is that there is a lesson that we should have learned in a previous life and didn't, that there is a lesson to learn that we need more than one life for, or simply that we didn't have time to heal a curse, a contract, or a trauma, from a previous life and to free ourselves from it in the period between one existence and another.

Generational karmic curses resemble karmic contracts in that they were also created in a past life, and they continue to affect the present life. However, there is a difference: karmic contracts are made of one's own volition, and generational karmic curses are inherited from other people. These curses are psychic attacks that can last for many lifetimes if they are not broken.

There are energetic cords that can link us to ancestors we never knew, places we have never lived in, or visited, and events we have not experienced in this current life. There are ancestral karmic contracts that were inherited from our ancestors without us having participated in their choice. Such ancestral contracts generate fears and expectation that the fears, or the will of an ancestor, will come true.

Sometimes we have energetic cords that come from past lives. If a traumatic event from a past life becomes repetitive over many lifetimes, energetic cords are formed that transcend several existences creating a powerful cord that breaks that person's ability to eliminate that traumatic pattern. Often all the traumas we suffer in our current life are small pieces of past life traumas.

Anyone who has lived through a traumatic event in one or more past lives, without overcoming it, lives their present in the expectation of reliving it. These people create new experiences on a subconscious level in the early years of their lives with the intention of traumatizing themselves and renewing their expectations. Usually the most common form of manifestation of these energy cords is through fears and phobias.

Another form of energetic cord is the one formed with beliefs. All the beliefs we have, positive or negative, have an energetic cord that unfolds from our being to the universal thought scheme of belief. Collective thinking is a product of the thoughts, emotions, and energies of all people who have ever held, or still hold, a specific belief, or who have collaborated with it.

When our thoughts and emotions are closely related to a specific belief in an acute and permanent way, we connect to that collective thought pattern, which feeds and reinforces our energetic cord with belief.

We often have toxic energy cords with various objects with which we have held emotional ties, among which are usually letters, books, photographs, paintings, clothes, shoes, etc.

If the relationship with the people who own, or associate, these objects ended on bad terms, the resentment that you, or other people, feel, is instantly transferred to the objects. It is not enough to cut the energetic cord with the objects, you must clean them. But in the best of cases, throw them away.

All the family antiques that are passed down from generation to generation accumulate the energies of all the people who owned them, or had contact with them. By possessing them you create energetic cords with those people, their traumas, and the experiences they lived.

It is healthy to sell, give away or throw away these objects, since when you break the physical bond, you automatically cut the energetic cord that binds you to them.

In the spiritual world we are the set of lives we have lived, even though we do not have memories of the events, or experiences, that we live.

For the soul there is neither space nor time. The soul can accumulate all the experiences we have lived in all our past lives. The person you are today is the sum of all your past lives.

Evil Eye, Curses and Envy

The evil eye, curses, and envy fall into the category of psychic attacks. They all happen when a person sends you strong vibrations where the main ingredient is negative energies. This can happen consciously, or unconsciously, but due to the intensity of these, they are very harmful.

The evil eye, curses and envy are much more serious when you maintain a relationship with that person, since the energetic cord that is created allows them full access to your energy.

However, there can also be energetic cords between people who are unknown, regardless of the limits of time, because energy can transcend time and space and reach any person or object with concentration and intention.

Psychic Possessions

Psychic possessions are common, but sometimes they go unnoticed. They occur when a spirit of low vibration, or a wandering soul, takes over a person's body causing changes in behavior and diseases. That entity penetrates through the aura.

When a person decides to free himself from that spirit, it is especially important that he chooses someone who is professional. If the person who is doing the work only limits himself to expelling the spirit, he will look for another body to lodge in.

The symptoms of psychic possession are completely different from the symptoms of other types of energetic attacks. Among them are emotional apathy, destructive behaviors, aggressiveness, memory loss, hearing voices, and physical changes in the possessed person.

Lucky dates to get married in 2025:

January 2, 10 and 25

February 1, 2, 9 and 26

March 5 & 6

April 2, 8 & 20

May 2, 8 and 28

June 1, 6, 20 and 22

July 2, 3, 10 and 27

August 1, 12 and 15

September 2, 20 and 24

October 1, 3, 16 and 25

Lucky Days for Rituals 2025

January

January 1: New Year's Day (Spiritual Reflection, Intention Setting) Perform spiritual baths and energetic cleansings.

January 14: New Moon in Capricorn (great for setting goals and grounding energy). Rituals for money.

January 15: Perfect day for love rituals.

January 25: Full Moon in Leo (Focus on Self-Expression and Creativity) Rituals for Health.

February

February 12: New Moon in Aquarius (Innovation and community focus) Love rituals.

February 19: Practice money rituals.

February 24: Full Moon in Virgo (Healing Energy, Focus on Health, and Order) Health Rituals.

March

March 2: New Moon in Pisces (Greater intuition and emotional sensitivity) Health rituals and spiritual baths.

March 6: rituals of love and health.

March 14: Full Moon in Libra (Balance, Relationships, and Harmony) March 20: Spring Equinox, Light and Dark Balance, Rebirth Energy)

March 21: Money rituals.

April

April 1: Easter Sunday.

April 6: New Moon in Aries (New Beginnings, Bravery, and Taking Action) Money Rituals.

April 14: Full Moon in Scorpio (Intense transformation, letting go of old patterns) love rituals.

April 20: Solar Eclipse (New Moon in Taurus - Manifestation of abundance and stability) money rituals.

May

May 5: Love rituals.

May 7: New Moon in Taurus (earthly and grounding energy for manifestation) Money rituals.

May 14: Health rituals.

May 23: Full Moon in Sagittarius (Adventure, search for truth, expansion) Rituals and energetic cleansings.

June

June 5: New Moon in Gemini (Communication, learning, curiosity) Love rituals.

June 13: Rituals of love.

June 21: Summer Solstice. Longest day of the year, celebration of abundance and growth (Pagan, Wiccan, Druid). Money rituals.

June 22: Full Moon in Capricorn (Hard Work, Discipline and Goal Achievement) Money rituals.

July

July 5 New Moon in Cancer (Parenting, home, emotional well-being) Rituals and love.

9 July: Rituals for health.

July 10: Full Moon in Aquarius (Rebellion, freedom, and individuality).

August

August 5: New Moon in Leo (Creativity, Leadership and Self-Confidence) Rituals for Money.

August 12: Peak of the Perseid meteor shower (Powerful energy for desires and manifestations. Any ritual.

August 14: Full Moon in Pisces (Spirituality, compassion, and dreams).

August 23: Lunar Eclipse - (Full Moon in Pisces) Emotional release, greater intuition. Love rituals.

September

September 5: New Moon in Virgo (Health, Organization and Clarity) Health rituals.

September 10: Money rituals.

September 21: Full Moon in Aries (Bold action, courage, start of new projects) Love rituals.

September 23: Autumn equinox. Day and night balance, harvest energy, introspection (pagan, Wiccan, druid) Energy cleansings.

October

October 5 New Moon in Libra (Focus on Relationships, Balance, and Diplomacy) Love Rituals.

October 14: Solar Eclipse - (New Moon in Libra) Readjustment of relationship dynamics and inner harmony.

October 20: Health rituals.

October 23: Full Moon in Taurus (Focus on Security, Values, and Stability) Money Rituals

November

November 1: Samhain (Pagan, Wiccan, Druid) - Honoring ancestors, death and rebirth, spiritual communication. Money rituals.

November 3: New Moon in Scorpio (Deep transformation, liberation, and rebirth).

November 12: Health rituals.

November 19: Full Moon in Gemini (Learning, Communication and Flexibility) Love rituals.

December

December 5: New Moon in Sagittarius (Optimism, Adventure, and Search for Truth) Money rituals.

December 8: Money rituals.

December 21: Winter solstice. The Longest Night, Introspection, Renewal (Pagan, Wiccan, Druid) Money Rituals.

December 24: Full Moon in Cancer (Emotional Connections, Home, and Family) Health Rituals.

December 25: Christmas.

December 31: Rituals to look forward to the new year 2026.

Lunar Calendar 2025

January 2025

Full Moon
1/13/2025
Cancer

New Moon
1/29/2025
Aquarius

29	30	31	1	2	3	4
5	6	7	8	9	10	11
12	13	14	15	16	17	18
19	20	21	22	23	24	25
26	27	28	29	30	31	1

Gemini, Predictions and Rituals 2025/Rubi

Full Moon 2/12/2025 Leo — February 2025 — New Moon 2/27/2025 Pisces

2	27	28	29	30	31	1
2	3	4	5	6	7	8
9	10	11	12	13	14	15
1	17	18	19	20	21	22
2	24	25	26	27	28	1

Full Moon 3/14/2025 Virgo — March 2025 — New Moon 3/29/2025 Aries

2	24	25	26	27	28	1
2	3	4	5	6	7	8
9	10	11	12	13	14	15
1	17	18	19	20	21	22
2	24	25	26	27	28	29
3	31	1	2	3	4	5

Gemini, Predictions and Rituals 2025/Rubi

04/12/2025 Full Moon Libra		April 2025			04/27/2025 New Moon Taurus	
3	31	1	2	3	4	5
6	7	8	9	10	11	12
1	14	15	16	17	18	19
2	21	22	23	24	25	26
2	28	29	30	1	2	3

Gemini, Predictions and Rituals 2025/Rubi

05/12/2025 Full Moon Scorpio		May 2025			05/25/2025 New Moon Gemini	
27	28	29	30	1	2	3
4	5	6	7	8	9	10
11	12	13	14	15	16	17
18	19	20	21	22	23	24
25	26	27	28	29	30	31

109

Gemini, Predictions and Rituals 2025/Rubi

Full Moon 06/11/2025 Sagittarius		June 2025			New Moon 06/25/2025 Cancer	
1	2	3	4	5	6	7
8	9	10	11	12	13	14
15	16	17	18	19	20	21
22	23	24	25	26	27	28
29	30	1	2	3	4	5

Gemini, Predictions and Rituals 2025/Rubi

07/10/2025 Full Moon Capricorn		July 2025			07/24/2025 New Moon Leo	
29	30	**1**	**2**	**3**	**4**	**5**
6	**7**	**8**	**9**	**10** 🌕	**11**	**12**
13	**14**	**15**	**16**	**17**	**18**	**19**
20	**21**	**22**	**23**	**24** 🌑	**25**	**26**
27	**28**	**29**	**30**	**31**	1	2

111

August 2025

08/09/2025 Full Moon Aquarius

08/23/2025 New Moon Virgo

2	28	29	30	31	**1**	**2**
3	**4**	**5**	**6**	**7**	**8**	**9**
1	**11**	**12**	**13**	**14**	**15**	**16**
1	**18**	**19**	**20**	**21**	**22**	**23**
2	**25**	**26**	**27**	**28**	**29**	**30**
3	1	2	3	4	5	6

09/07/2025 Full Moon Pisces Eclipse	September 2025					New Moon 09/21/2025 Virgo Eclipse
31	1	2	3	4	5	6
7	8	9	10	11	12	13
14	15	16	17	18	19	20
21	22	23	24	25	26	27
28	29	30	1	2	3	4

10/06/2025 Full Moon Aries			October 2025			10/21/2025 New Moon Scorpio	
28	29	30	1	2	3	4
5	6	7	8	9	10	11
12	13	14	15	16	17	18
19	20	21	22	23	24	25
26	27	28	29	30	31	1

Gemini, Predictions and Rituals 2025/Rubi

11/05/2025 Full Moon Taurus		November 2025			11/20/2025 New Moon Sagittarius	
2	27	28	29	30	31	1
2	3	4	5	6	7	8
9	10	11	12	13	14	15
1	17	18	19	20	21	22
2	24	25	26	27	28	29
3	1	2	3	4	5	6

Gemini, Predictions and Rituals 2025/Rubi

12/04/2025 Full Moon Gemini		December 2025				12/19/2025 New Moon Sagittarius	
30	1	2	3	4	5	6
7	8	9	10	11	12	13
14	15	16	17	18	19	20
21	22	23	24	25	26	27
28	29	30	31	1	2	3

Full Moon Calendar 2025

Wolf Moon   Saturday, January 11
Snow Moon   Monday, February 10
Worm Moon   Wednesday, March 12
Pink Moon   Thursday, April 10
Flower Moon   Saturday, May 10
Strawberry   Moon Monday, June 9
Deer Moon   Tuesday, July 8
Sturgeon   Moon Thursday, August 7
Harvest   Moon Friday, September 5
Hunter's   Moon Sunday, October 5
Beaver   Moon Monday, November 3
Cold Moon   Wednesday, December 3

Energy Cleanses by 2025

Bath to Open Your Paths 2025

*You must do this bath the first week of the year.

For the year to be positive, this bath is beneficial.

Boil rue, bay leaf, mint, basil, saraguey rosemary break and nine white flowers. When it cools down, you put honey on it and mix it with more water in your bathtub. You immerse yourself in that powerful bath for 15 minutes. When you go out, do not dry yourself with the towel.

If you wish, you can use it to clean your home or office, always cleaning in the direction of the front door of the place.

*Search on Google what other names the Saraguey breaker has in your country.

Lucky Bath

This bath is special if you want to succeed in something specific. Look for a bouquet of the chamomile plant, two tablespoons of honey, a cinnamon stick, and two oranges. You boil all these ingredients and when the mixture cools down, you pour it into your bathtub. You must do it for three consecutive days.

*Choose from these baths the ones you need, according to your situation so that you start the year energetically purified.

Blockage's Removal Bath

In a bowl add nine tablespoons of honey, cinnamon and nine tablespoons of sugar. You mix it very well, let it rest in the moonlight, and the next day you bathe in this mixture.

Bath to Attract Harmony in the Home

Boil a Rosemary plant, cinnamon cloves, and basil with holy water or moon water. You put it to cool and add Lavender essential oil.

You throw it in your bathtub, immerse yourself for 15 minutes and that is it.

Bath Against Envy

If you want to cut the evil eye, or envy, you must boil eight lemons, three tablespoons of honey, three tablespoons of sugar, in three liters of water. When it gets a little cold, mix it with water in your bathtub and immerse yourself for half an hour.

Bath against Negativity

Need:

Five rosemary leaves

Chamomile

Three leaves of rue

One basil leaf,

3 Laurel Branches

Three sprigs of thyme

Sea Salt

Seven black peppers

Cumin

One cinnamon sprig

One tablespoon honey

Boil all the ingredients, except the honey and salt, for 5 minutes. When it cools down, add the honey and salt. Take a bath with this mixture for three consecutive days and you will not only drive away negative energies, but you will attract abundance into your life.

Bath to Attract Money

Need:

Seven different colored flowers

Seven tablespoons honey

Seawater or rain

Three coconut waters

One container

Three drops of your favorite perfume

In the container you place the petals of the flowers and the rainwater or seawater. Then you add the drops of perfume and coconut water. You mix everything together and bathe for a week with this mystical water.

Every time you use this spiritual bath you repeat aloud: I am a prosperous person, who has wealth and abundance. The paths of money are clear for me, and I receive everything that belongs to me in the Universe.

Curse Bath

Need:

Four rosemary leaves

Three leaves of rue

Two bay leaves

1 Artemis leaf

You mix all these leaves with water and let it sit overnight.

The next day you bathe in this mixture, or you will be free of all curses.

Aphrodisiac bath

Need:

Five petals of Rosa

Five leaves or sprigs of rosemary

Five thyme leaves

5 Basil Leaf

5 Jasmine Flowers

You boil all the ingredients and bathe with that water before sleeping, do not dry you with the towel.

Beauty Bath

Need:

5 Lavender Leaves

Five rosemary leaves

Three mint leaves

One lily flower

Seven thyme leaves

You must crush all these plants, with a little water so that it is easier for you, and you can make it like a paste.

When you bathe you smear it all over your body, stay like this for 15 minutes. Then rinse, but do not towel dry.

Bath to Restore Energies and Vitality

Need:

9 Carnation Sheets

9 Lavender Leaves

Nine rosemary leaves

Nine basil leaves

Boil all the leaves for 5 minutes, stir the mixture clockwise. When it cools down, use it. This bath gives you strength, you must do it for three consecutive days.

Bath to Attract Love

Need:

Three red rose petals

Three mint leaves

Four sprigs of Parsley

Mix these ingredients together and place them in your favorite perfume or cologne. Pour it on yourself daily so that love comes into your life.

Bath to Get Fast Money

Need:

Three rosemary leaves

Two basil leaves

Cinnamon

Three mint leaves

Bathe in this mixture after boiling it for 30 minutes. Do not dry yourself with the towel.

Bath for Material Prosperity

Need:

Three cloves

Two parsley leaves

One rue leaf

Bathe in this mixture after boiling it for 30 minutes. Do not dry yourself with the towel.

Bath for Spiritual Peace

Need:

Three petals of Girasol

Two red rose petals

3 Jasmine

Spray your body with this water after you have mixed all these ingredients. Do not dry yourself with the towel.

Bath for Protection against Envy

Need:

Seven rosemary leaves

Three bay leaves

Two basil leaves

Star anise

One leaf of Rompe Saraguey

Bathe in this mixture for five consecutive days. Do not dry yourself with the towel.

Bath to Attract Success

Need:

Nine sunflower petals

Nine red roses

Nine pink roses

Nine white roses

Two branches of rue

Four oranges

Nine basil leaves

One golden candle

One bundle of cloves

One large container

Yellow Paper

You must boil water for 10 minutes and then add the components in this order: sunflowers, rue, basil leaves, orange, and cloves. Stir it for 3 minutes and let it cool. Before you start bathing, light the candle. While you take a bath, you ask your guardian angel to envelop you in his light and open your paths. Do not dry yourself with the towel.

You finish by wrapping the waste in the paper and leaving it outside your house.

Bath for Instant Luck

Need:

rue

basil

rosemary

chamomile

cinnamon

honey

You should prepare a mixture with these ingredients on a Friday at Venus Time. Boil them for 5 minutes and let them rest. Then you bathe from head to toe and while you do so you repeat in your mind: "I am lucky and power" Do not dry yourself with the towel.

Bath for Good Luck

Need:

Cinnamon stick

Eight basil leaves

Nine rosemary leaves

Nine thyme leaves

Boil all the ingredients, then put it in the light of the Full Moon. The next day you bathe in this mixture. Do not dry yourself with the towel.

Bath to Attract Love

Need:

Cundiamor

Basil

Mint

Sunflower

Verbena

Three yellow flowers.

Place all the ingredients inside a glass container. Leave it exposed to the Sun and Moon for three days and three nights. Then you take a bath with this mixture. Do not dry yourself with the towel.

Bath to Be Attractive

Mix four roses, four lilies, cinnamon, red apple peel, and mint in a bowl of rainwater. You leave it exposed for 2 nights to the moonlight. The next day you strain it and bathe in this water. Do not dry yourself with the towel.

Bath to Recover a Love

Need:

Seven mint leaves.

Four marjoram leaves.

Four orange leaves

Six verbena leaves

Two cloves

Alcohol

You must crush all the plants, extract the juice by squeezing them. You prepare an infusion with the cloves, and when it cools down you add plant extract and alcohol. After your normal bath, you pour that infusion over your body. Do not dry yourself with the towel.

Bath to Eliminate the Evil Eye

Need:

River water

Seawater.

Rainwater.

Rue

Mix the three waters with the rue and boil it. When it cools down, put it in a container and bathe for three consecutive days with the mixture.

Do not dry yourself with the towel.

Bath to Attract Abundance

Need:

Parsley Branches.

Sage Sticks

Branches of Rompe Saraguey.

Five yellow roses.

Bee honey.

One green candle

Crush all the plants with water, add honey and leave this mixture exposed to the Sun and the Moon for an entire day.

You divide it into three parts and store it in a glass container. You light the green candle and for three consecutive days you bathe in the mixture. Do not dry yourself with the towel.

Rituals for January

Ritual for money

Need:

-Ice
- Holy Water, the Blessed
- Corn kernels
- Sea salt
- 1 clay container
- Three green floating candles
- Cartridge or parchment paper and pencil
- 1 new sewing needle

Write your requests about money on the paper, then sign your name on the candles with the needle. To cleanse your energy, you will use the clay container where you will place the ice and the sacred water, in equal proportions you add three handfuls of sea salt.

Introduce both hands into the casserole so you will be expelling the negative energies that you have inside you. Take your hands out of the water, but do not dry them.

Add a handful of corn to the container and put your hands back in for three minutes. The last thing you will do is light the candles with wooden matches and place them inside the container. With the fire of the three candles, you burn the paper with your desires, and you will let the candles burn out.

The remains of this spell you bury somewhere where the Sun can give it, because in this way your desire will continue to receive energies.

Spell for good energies and prosperity

Need:

– 1 sheet of blue paper

- Sea salt

- 1 plated-large candle

- 3 rose incenses

- 16 small white candles

Form a circle on the sheet of paper with the salt. On top of the circle made with the salt, he structures two circles, one with the five small candles and another on the outside with the remaining eleven. Place the silver candle in the middle. You light the candles in the following order: first, those in the inner circle, then those in the outer circle, and finally the one in the middle.

You should light the incense with the larger candle and put it in a container outside the circles. As you perform this operation, visualize your wishes for prosperity and success. Finally, let all the candles burn out. You can throw the remains in the trash.

Ritual for Love

Need:

- 1 Orange
- Red pen
- Gold paper
- 1 red candle
- 7 new sewing needles
- Red ribbon
- Yellow tape

You cut the orange in two and in the middle place the gold paper where you will have previously signed your name five times and that of the person you love with red tint.

Close the orange with the paper inside and hold it with the sewing needles.

Then you roll it up with the yellow and red ribbon, it should be enthralled. You light the red candle and place the orange candle in front of it.

While performing this ritual, repeat aloud: "Love reigns in my heart, I am forever united to (you repeat the name of the person), no one will separate us."

When the candle burns out, you should bury the orange in your yard or in a park, preferably where there are flowers.

Spell to Make Someone Think of You

Get a mirror that women use to put on makeup and place a photograph of yourself behind the mirror. Then you take a photograph of the person you want to think of yourself and place it face down in front of the mirror (so that the two photos are looking at each other with the mirror between them). Wrap the mirror with a piece of red cloth and tie it with a red thread so that they are secure, and the photographs cannot move. This should be placed under your bed and well hidden.

Spell to Preserve Good Health

Necessary elements.
- 1 white candle.
- 1 card of the Angel of your devotion.
- 3 sandalwood incenses.
- Charcoals.
- Dried eucalyptus and basil herbs.
- A handful of rice, a handful of wheat.
- 1 white plate or a tray.
- 8 Rose petals.
- 1 perfume bottle, personal.
- 1 wooden box.

You should clean the environment by lighting the charcoals in a metal container. When the coals are well lit, you will gradually place the dried herbs in them and go around the room with the container, so that the negative energies are eliminated. Once the incense is finished, you must open the windows so that the smoke dissipates. Set up an altar on a table covered with a white tablecloth. Place the chosen card on top of it and place the three incense pieces around it in the shape of a triangle. You must consecrate the white candle, then light it and place it in front of the angel along with the perfume uncovered.

You must be relaxed, for that you must concentrate on your breathing. Visualize your angel and thank him for all the good health you have and will always have, this gratitude must come from the depths of your heart.

After you have thanked him, you will give him as an offering the handful of rice and the handful of wheat, which you must place inside the white tray or plate.

On the altar you sprinkle all the rose petals, giving thanks for the favors received.
After you finish thanking you, you will leave the candle lit until it is completely consumed. The last thing you should do is gather all the remains of the candle, incense sticks, rice, and wheat, and place them in a plastic bag and you will throw it in a place where there are trees without the bag.

You put the image of the angel and the rose petals inside the box and place them in a safe place in your house. The energized perfume you use when you feel that the energies are going down, while visualizing your angel and asking for their protection. This ritual is most effective if you perform it on a Thursday or Monday at Jupiter or Moon time.

Rituals for February

Ritual with Honey to Attract Prosperity.

Need:

- 1 white candle

- 1 blue candle

- 1 green sail

- 3 Amethysts.

- One-fourth liter of pure honey

-Rosemary.

- 1 new sewing needle

On a Monday, at the time of the Moon, he writes on the green candle the symbol of money ($), on the white candle a pentacle and on the blue candle the astrological symbol of the planet Jupiter. Then, cover them with honey and spread the cinnamon and rosemary on them, in that order. Then place them in the shape of a pyramid, with the top tip being the green candle, the left the blue candle and the right the white candle. Next to each candle you place an amethyst. Turn them on and ask your spirit guides or guardian angel for material prosperity. You will see the tremendous results.

To Attract Impossible Love

Need:

- 1 red rose
- 1 white rose
- 1 red candle
- 1 white candle
- 3 yellow candles
- Glass fountain
- Pentacle #4 of Venus

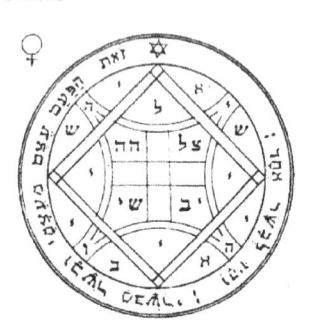

You should place the yellow candles in the shape of a triangle. You write on the back of the pentacle of Venus your desires about love and the name of that person you want in your life, you place the fountain on top of the pentacle in the middle. You light the red, white candles, and put them in the dish along with the roses. You repeat this phrase: "Universe diverts into my heart the light of love from (full name)." You repeat it three times. When the candles have gone out, you take everything to the yard and bury it.

Ritual for Health

Spell for Chronic Pain.

Necessary Elements:

- 1 golden candle
- 1 white candle
- 1 green candle
- 1 Tourmaline Black person
- 1 photo of yourself or personal item
- 1 glass of moon water
- Photograph of the person or personal object

Place the three candles in the shape of a triangle and place the photo or personal object in the center. You put the glass of moon water on top of the photo and pour the tourmaline inside.

Then you light the candles and repeat the following incantation: "I light this candle to achieve my recovery, invoking my inner fires and the protective salamanders and undines, to transmute this pain and discomfort into healing energy of health and well-being.

Repeat this sentence three times. When you finish the prayer take the glass, take out the tourmaline and throw the water into a drain in the house, blow out the candles with your fingers and keep them to repeat this spell until you fully recover. Tourmaline can be used as a health charm.

Rituals for March

Pepper to Attract Money.

Need:

- 7 peppercorns
- 7 rue leaves.
- 7 grains coarse sea salt
- 1 small red cloth bag.
- 1 red ribbon
- 1 citrine quartz

Insert all the ingredients into the baggie. Close it with the red ribbon and leave it exposed overnight to the light of the Full Moon. Then sleep nine days with it under your pillow. You must carry it with you in an invisible place on your body.

Ritual with Oil for Love

Need:

- Almond oil
- 7 drops of lemon oil
- 7 basil leaves
- 7 apple seeds
- 7 tangerine seeds
- 1 small dark crystal knob

You must mix all the oils in a glass dish with a wooden spoon. Then add the basil leaves and the crushed tangerine and apple seeds. Let the mixture sit outside for a Full Moon night. The next day you strain the preparation and pour it into a dark glass jar with a lid. It is for personal use.

Spell to improve health.

You should get a white candle, a green candle, and a yellow candle.
You will consecrate them (from the base to the wick) with pine essence and place them on a table with a light blue tablecloth, in the shape of a triangle.

In the center, you will put a small glass container with alcohol and a small amethyst.

At the base of the container, a paper with the name of the sick person or a photo with their full name on the back and date of birth.
You light the three candles and leave them lit until they are completely consumed. While performing this ritual, visualize the person completely healthy.

Rituals for April

Bath for Good Luck.

Need:

- Metal Casserole- 3 crushed lemons
- 1 tablespoon brown sugar
- Full Moon Water

Mix the ingredients and boil them for 10 minutes. Then pour this mixture into hot water in a bathtub and take a bath for at least 15 minutes. You can also rinse with it if you do not have a tub.

Ritual to Earn Money.

Cut a lemon in half and squeeze the two halves, leaving only the two lids. You do not need lemon juice; you can give it another use. Insert three ordinary coins inside one of the halves, close them and with a piece of gold ribbon roll them up. Bury it in a pot with a lottery plant. Take care of the plant with love. Let the candles burn out completely and keep the coins in your wallet; these three coins you cannot spend. When the bay leaf and rosemary dry the burns, and you pass the smoke of this incense through your home or business.

Ritual for love

This ritual is most effective if you perform it during the phase of the Gibbous Crescent Moon and on a Friday at Venus Earth Time.

Need:
- 1 tablespoon honey
- 1 Pentacle #5 of Venus.
- 1 pen with red ink
- 1 white candle
- 1 new sewing needle

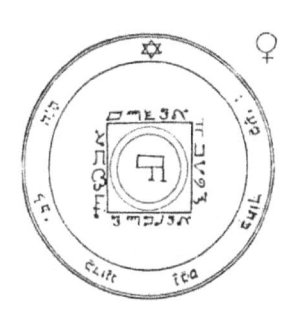

Pentacle #5 of Venus.

You should write on the back of the pentacle of Venus in red ink the full name of the person you love and how you want them to behave towards you, you should be specific. Then you dip it in the honey and roll it into the candle so that it sticks. You secure it with the sewing needle. When the candle is burnt out, bury the remains and repeat aloud: "The love of (name) belongs to me alone."

Spell against Depression

You should pick up a fig with your right hand and place it on the left side of your mouth without chewing or swallowing it. Then you pick a grape with your left hand and place it on the right side of your mouth without chewing it.

When you already have both fruits in your mouth you bite them at the same time and swallow them, the fructose they emanate will give you energy and joy.

African Aphrodisiac

You should soak six vanilla seed pods in tequila for two weeks in an airtight bottle.

Shake it times a day and when you need it, drink between ten to fifteen drops to stimulate your sex drive.

Mint

Mint is an aromatic and medicinal plant. It is popular for its benefits, and for a variety of uses.

Peppermint provides your body with proteins, potassium, magnesium, calcium, phosphorus, vitamin C, iron, and vitamin A. In addition, it is used in the treatment of asthma, to improve digestion, in skin care, for nausea and headaches.

This plant has ascorbic acid, which eases the expulsion of mucus, and acts as a natural antitussive.

Its magical properties have been accepted since ancient times. Its fame comes from ancient Greece and Rome, where it was related to the gods of healing and prosperity. They said that carrying mint in talismans or burning it as incense attracted fortune.

Peppermint in the Middle Ages was used in love spells because it was believed to arouse passion and strengthen romantic bonds.

This plant has protective properties and is used to create a magical shield against the evil eye or witchcraft. It is used to ward off negative energies and increase the ability to concentrate.

Rosemary

Rosemary is used to treat vertigo and epilepsy. Stress and chronic diseases can also be treated with rosemary. It is especially useful for calming anxiety, depression, and insomnia.

Rosemary has antiseptic, antibacterial and antifungal properties that help improve the immune system. It helps to improve and is used to treat migraines and other types of headaches.

Rosemary when you burn it emits powerful purifying vibrations, which is why it is used to cleanse and get rid of negative energies.

When you place it under your pillow it guarantees you dreams without nightmares. In spiritual baths it purifies.

Rosemary is used in the incense of love and sexual desires.

Garlic

Garlic has esoteric and medicinal properties. It serves as an expectorant, antispasmodic, antiseptic, and antimicrobial.

Garlic is a powerful charm for abundance. garlic cloves, fastened with a red ribbon, should be placed behind the front door of your house to create a shield against scarcity.

In the same way that salt acts as a protector or vinegar as a blocker, garlic has been shown to be the most efficient neutralizer and purifier for bad energies. The ancient magicians recommended it in all their formulas.

Garlic is considered a symbol of prosperity and as an amulet it can attract money.

Since ancient times it has been used to ward off demons, spirits, and mythical vampires.

It is advisable to take a bath with boiled and strained garlic cloves. This water is applied to the head and drives away depressive states.

Rituals for May

Ritual to Attract Money Instantly.

Need:

- 5 cinnamon sprigs
- 1 dried orange peel
- 1 liter of holy water
- 1 green sail

Put the cinnamon, orange peel and liter of water to boil, then let the mixture rest until it cools. Pour the liquid into a spray. Light the candle in the northern part of the living room of your house and spray all the rooms while repeating: "Angel of Abundance, I invoke your presence in this house so that nothing is missing, and we will always have more than we need." When you finish, thank you three times and leave the candle burning. You can do it on a Sunday or Thursday at the time of the planet Venus or Jupiter.

Spell to Attract Your Soulmate

Need:

- Rosemary leaves
- Parsley leaves
- Basil leaves
- Metal casserole
- 1 red heart-shaped candle
- Cinnamon essential oil
- 1 heart drawn on a red paper
- Alcohol
- Lavender oil

You must first consecrate the candle with cinnamon oil, then light it and place it next to the metal casserole. Mix all the plants in the casserole. You write on the paper heart all the characteristics of the person you want in your life; you write the details. Add five drops of the lavender oil to the paper and place it inside the casserole dish. Spray it with the alcohol and set it on fire. All the remains must be scattered on the seashore, while you do so concentrate and ask for that person to come into your life.

Ritual for Health

Need:

Six rosemary leaves

6 Lavender Leaves

Six petals of white roses

Six mint leaves

One palo of cinnamon

Boil all the ingredients and let them sit overnight, if possible, in the light of the Full Moon.

The next day you bathe with the mixture, do not dry yourself with the towel, let your body absorb these energies.

Rituals for June

Ritual to Attract More Money.

Need:

- 3 tablespoons tea
- 3 tablespoons thyme
- 1 pinch nutmeg
- 3 coals
- 1 metal casserole with handles
- 1 little core

Place the coals in the casserole dish, turn them on and add the other ingredients. When the fire has gone out, arrange the remains in the small box, and keep it in your room for eleven days. Then bury it in a pot or in your backyard. You should start this ritual on a Thursday.

Ritual to Consolidate Love

This spell is most effective in the Full Moon phase.

Need:

- 1 wooden box
- Photographs
- Honey
- Red rose petals
- 1 amethyst quartz
- Cinnamon stick

You must take the photographs, print the full names and dates of birth, place them inside the box so that they are facing each other. Add the honey, rose petals, amethyst, and cinnamon. You place the box under your bed for thirteen days. After this time, extract the amethyst from the box, wash it with moon water. You must keep it with you as an amulet to attract that love you crave. The rest you must take to a river or a forest.

Protective Bath before a Surgical Operation

Necessary elements.

- Purple Bell

- Coconut Water
- Husk
- Cologne 1800
- Always Alive
- Mint Leaves
- Rue leaves
- Rosemary leaves
- White Candle
- Lavender Oil

This bath is most effective if you do it on a Thursday at the time of the Moon or Mars.

Boil all the plants in the coconut water, when it cools down strain it and add the husk, cologne, lavender oil, and light the candle in the west part of your Bath.

You pour the mixture into the bath water. If you do not have a bathtub, you throw it on yourself and do not dry yourself.

Rituals for July

Cleaning the Business for Prosperity.

Need:

- Basil leaves

- 7 cloves of garlic

- Rosemary leaves

- Sage leaves

- 7 rue leaves

- 7 mint leaves

-Oregano

- 7 parsley leaves

- Sea salt

- 10 liters of holy water or Full Moon water

Simmer all the ingredients for a period of one hour. When it is cool, strain it out and distribute seven tablespoons of this liquid to the inside and outside corners of your business for nine days straight. You should always start this ritual at the time of the planet Venus or Jupiter.

Romani Ritual

You take a red candle and consecrate it with sunflower oil. You print the full name of the person you want to keep. Then you cover it with brown sugar. When the candle has enough sugar attached, cut off the tip and light it underneath, that is, the other way around. As you light the candle you repeat in your mind: "By lighting this candle I am igniting the passion of (you say person's name) so that our relationship will be sweeter than sugar." When the candle burns out, you must bury it, but before closing the hole, sprinkle a little cinnamon.

Bath for Good Health

Need:

Cinnamon stick

Eight basil leaves

Nine rosemary leaves

Nine thyme leaves

Boil all the ingredients, then put it in the light of the Full Moon. The next day you bathe in this mixture. Do not dry yourself with the towel.

Rituals for August

Ritual for Money

Need:

-Matches

- Sandalwood incense

- 1 silver candle, in the shape of a pyramid.

Light the incense and spread the smoke to every corner of your house. Leave the incense lit and light the silver candle. Focus on your order for a while until you visualize it.

Repeat the following sentence, three times: "New Moon, give me strength to face my economic problems, you are my guide to find prosperity and money. I receive your powerful energy with gratitude." Then you must let the candle, and the incense, burn out completely. You can dispose of the remains in the trash.

Spell to Transform you into a Magnet.

To have a magnetic aura and attract women, or men, you must make a yellow bag having the heart of a white dove and the eyes of a powdered turtle. This bag must be carried in your right pocket if you are a man. Women will wear this same pouch, but inside the bra on the left side.

Bath for Health

Need:

River water

Seawater.

Rainwater.

Rue

Mix the three waters with the rue and boil it. When it cools down, put it in a container and bathe for three consecutive days with the mixture.

Do not dry yourself with the towel.

Bamboo

Bamboo is a plant with great spiritual significance, and it has excellent value, not only for its practical uses, but also for its spiritual symbolism. It is linked to resilience and humility.

Bamboo, in Japanese culture, symbolizes life and death since this plant blooms, and generates seeds only once in its life.

Bamboo is used against the evil eye. Record your wishes on a piece of Bamboo and bury it in a secluded place, they will be fulfilled at once.

In traditional Chinese medicine, Bamboo is used for problems of the bones, joints, and skin. From the nodes of the bamboo stem, a substance called "bamboosil" is extracted, which is an essential element for the proper functioning of our bone tissue and skin.

Pumpkin

The ancient Egyptians considered the Pumpkin a symbol of good luck, the Greeks claim that pumpkins are a symbol of fertility and economic solvency.

In the Middle Ages, pumpkins were considered symbols of prosperity.

Pumpkins are linked to prosperity, and they are also considered symbols of regeneration. It is quite common in the East to eat pumpkin seeds in rituals of spiritual transformation on the day of the spring equinox.

Pumpkin helps fight chronic diseases. Pumpkins are rich in alpha-carotene, beta-carotene, and beta-cryptoxanthin, all of which neutralize free radicals, and prevent damage to our cells.

Beta-carotene provides the body with the vitamin A we need, and vitamin A and beta-carotene have been proven to help prevent the risk of cataracts. Pumpkin is rich in vitamin C, which increases white blood cells in the body.

Eucalyptus

Eucalyptus has spiritual benefits. It is considered a natural way to help open the way when we are struggling.

Its aroma, refreshing and relaxing, offers inner peace, and helps to ward off negative energies. The smell of Eucalyptus stimulates concentration and helps us connect with our inner selves.

This plant relieves infections and respiratory diseases, disinfects the environment against viral processes, reduces inflammation in the skin, prevents skin dryness, and disinfects wounds.

It is balsamic and expectorant, as it stimulates the secretory cells of the bronchial mucosa.

If you boil eucalyptus leaves and spray your house, you will be transmuting the energies around you.

Parsley

Parsley is related to good luck, protection, health, and rituals to attract money.

The esoteric properties of Parsley have been known since ancient times. Homer in his work "Odyssey" mentioned Parsley.

The Greeks considered Parsley a sacred plant, and planted it as a condiment, and as a plant of good luck. Charlemagne had it planted in the gardens of his palace in the ninth century, becoming a fashion at the time.

The Greeks and Romans placed parsley crowns on their graves, and gladiators wore it in battles because it gave them cunning and strength.

Laurel

Since the times of the Greeks and Romans, the Laurel has played a key role in the esoteric and metaphysical world.

Kings, emperors, and nobles used a laurel wreath as a symbol of honor and fortune since the Laurel in their civilization was a divine plant with which the god Apollo was venerated.

The Laurel attracts money, and prosperity to those who have it. This plant is also used to make powerful energy cleansing rituals.

It is protective par excellence and is used as an amulet to drive away negative forces.

Rituals for September

To attract Material Abundance.

Need:
- 1 gold coin or a gold object, without stones.
- 1 copper coin
- 1 silver coin

During a Crescent Moon night with the coins in your hands, head to a place where the moon's rays illuminate them. With your hands up, you will repeat: "Luna, help me so that my fortune will always grow, and prosperity will always be with me." Make the coins ring inside your hands. Then you will keep them in your wallet. You can repeat this ritual every month.

Love Spell with Basil and Red Coral

Need:
- 1 Pot with a plant that has yellow flowers
- 1 Red Coral
- Basil leaves

- 1 Sheet of yellow paper
- 1 Red thread
- Cinnamon powder

You write on the paper your name and the name of the person you love. You fold it into four parts and wrap it with the basil leaves. You tie it with the red thread. You bury it in the pot and place the red coral on top. Before closing the hole, sprinkle the cinnamon. Every New Moon day you pour honey water on it.

Ritual for Health

Need:
-1 tablespoon of honey
-1 tablespoon white or apple cider vinegar

During the Waxing Moon, before you leave for work, and at the time of the planet Jupiter or Venus, wash your hands as your routine. Then rinse them with vinegar, pour honey on them and rinse them again, but do not dry them, while doing this ritual repeat in your mind: "Health will come and stay with me." Then he applauds, energetically.

Rituals for October

Ritual to Ensure Prosperity

Need:

- 1 Round table
- 1 Yellow cloth
- 3 golden candles
- 3 blue candles
- Wheat
- Rice

In a secluded and quiet place in your home, you will place a round table, which you will clean with vinegar. Place the yellow cloth on it. Light the three golden triangle-shaped candles starting with the candle at the tip in a clockwise direction. In the middle throw a handful of wheat and while you do so, visualize all the prosperity that your new business will bring you.

On the second night you place the three blue candles next to the golden candles, light them and where the wheat is, add a handful of rice. Focus your mind on your success.

When the candles are burned, you wrap everything in the yellow cloth and bury it.

Spell to Subdue in Love

Need:
- 1 dark glass bottle with lid
- Nails of the person to be mastered
- Rue leaves
-Cinnamon
- 3 black ribbons
- 1 magnet

You must put your nails, the magnet, the rue leaves, and the cinnamon inside the bottle. Cap the bottle and wrap it with the black ribbons. You bury it and when you seal the hole you must urinate on it.

Bath with Parsley for Health.

You must get parsley leaves, mint. Cinnamon and honey. Place the plants in a saucepan and let them cook for three minutes, without boiling.

Add the honey and cinnamon, then strain it. Bathe as you usually do, at the end of the bath, you pour the water you have prepared on your body, from the neck down, while thinking positively about attracting health to your body.

Energy Cleansing with an Egg

There are options for this procedure.
Need:

- 1 fresh egg, preferably white.
- 2 glass glasses with water, one normal, and one wider.
- 1 ceramic or glass container.
- Sea salt
- 1 white candle
- 1 incense
- 1 amulet, talisman, or protective quartz.

You take a separate glass container, put water, and add nine teaspoons of sea salt. You leave the eggs you are going to use inside for 5 minutes, and in the meantime take the wider glass and fill it with water. That glass is where you are going to crack the egg, at the right time.

You light the white candle, and the incense, next to the normal-sized glass, which you also must fill with water, and add three teaspoons of sea salt, so that it collects the negative energies that may result from the cleansing.

You put on protective quartz, amulet, shelter, or whatever else you use for magical and energetic protection.
When you are lighting the candle and incense, you ask for the help and protection of your spiritual teachers, guides, angels, protective ancestors, gods, or saints of your devotion.

Then you take the egg, and pass it all over the body and its contour making circles and repeating:

"Just as this egg passes through my body, it is cleansed of bad energies, evil eye, envy, and black magic works. May all the bad that I am dragging pass from my body to this egg, and may my aura be free from all filth and malignancy, obstacles or disease, and may the egg collect all that is bad."
You should accentuate the cleansing passes on specific areas of the body such as the head, forehead, chest, hands, stomach, above the genitals, feet, nape, cervical area and back.
Then you crack the egg into the glass you prepared for that and try to make a reading of the formations that occur in the water. You should do that after minutes.

About interpretation, the basic thing is that the yolk goes to the bottom of the glass when we break the egg. If it stays in the middle, or goes up, it is a negative signal.

A bloody yolk shows persistent bad energies, the evil eye, black magic works, or hexes. The egg can also be accompanied by formations of ascending peaks, and bubbles.
If bubbles come out surrounding the yolk towards the top, there is envy and negativity around you, which prevent you from moving forward. This may be causing physical discomfort, fatigue, and lack of energy.

If the yolk seems cooked, and the white is very white, it is likely that there are powerful negative energies lurking around you, works against you to close your paths, cause misfortune in your home, and sink your life. In that specific case, I at once send the person to the doctor for a general check-up.

Rituals for November

Ritual to Attract Fast Money.

Need:

- 1 legal tender banknote, regardless of its value.
- 1 container that is made of copper.
- 8 gold coins of legal tender or Chinese coins.
- 1 sprig dried basil
- Rice grains.
- 1 gold-colored bag
- 1 yellow ribbon
- 1 white chalk
- Coarse sea salt
- 9 golden candles.
- 9 green candles

You draw a circle with the white chalk, preferably in the courtyard (if you do not have this possibility, do it on the floor of a room with windows, so that they can stay open).

When midnight is past you should place the copper container in the middle of the circle, fold the bill into four equal parts, and place it inside the copper container. In this container you should also put the dried basil, rice, baggie, yellow ribbon, and eight coins. Around the container, inside the circle, you will place the nine green candles. Outside the circle you place the nine golden candles.

With the sea salt you will make a third circle outside the two rows of candles. Then you light the green candles, clockwise, as you repeat aloud the following incantation: "I ask the Sun to fill me with gold, I ask the Moon to fill me with silver, and the great planet Jupiter to flood me with riches."

When you finish the summoning, start lighting the golden candles, but this time counterclockwise, and repeat the earlier prayer.

When the candles have burned out, sweep all the waste towards the exit door, collect it, and put it in a nylon bag. This bag should be thrown away at a crossroads.
The rice, basil and the seven golden coins are put inside the bag and tied with the ribbon. This will serve as an amulet. The bill must be kept in your purse or wallet.

Ritual for the Union of Two Persons

Need:
- 1 change of underwear from each person (used)

- 1 magnet
- Palo Santo
- 8 rue leaves
- 2 pigeon eggs
- Agua sagrada
- 2 white pigeon feathers
- 1 medium-sized wooden box.
- 2 small cloth dolls (female and male)

You print the corresponding names on the cloth dolls. Place the two changes of clothes inside the box and the dolls on top in the shape of a cross.
You put the magnet in the center of this cross. On top you put the rue leaves, the two feathers and close the box. You splash it with the sacred water and the smoke of the Palo Santo passes through it. You bury it at the foot of a ceiba tree.

Shamanic Energy Cleansing

Shamanic energy cleansings use indigenous elements such as feathers, plant smoke, or resins. The use of sounds such as drumming, maracas, rattles also help by unblocking energy fields.
These cleanings are simple, the person is usually standing, or sitting, although it could be done in any position. It can be done on children, animals, objects, and spaces.

Need:
-   6 rosemary leaves

- 6 Lavender Leaves
- 6 petals of white roses
- 6 mint leaves
- 1 palo of cinnamon

You boil all the ingredients, and let them sit for a whole night, if possible, in the light of the Full Moon.
The next day you bathe with the mixture, do not dry yourself with the towel, let your body absorb these energies.

Rituals for December

Cash Flow Ritual

Need:
- 2 silver coins of any denomination
- 1 transparent glass container
- Agua Sagrada
- Sea salt
- Fresh leche
- Amethyst stone

Add the holy water and sea salt to the bowl. Place the coins in the water, and repeat in your mind, "You cleanse and purify yourself; you make me prosperous." Two days later you take the coins out of the water, go to the garden, and dig a hole and bury the coins and amethyst. If you do not have a garden, bury them somewhere where there is soil. When you have buried the coins, before closing the hole, pour the fresh milk on it. Think about the amount of money you want to get. Once you have expressed your wishes, you can cover the hole. Try to hide it as best as possible so that no one digs there again. At six weeks, dig up the coins and amethyst, always have them with you as amulets.

About The Authors

In addition to her astrological knowledge, Alina Rubi has an abundant professional education; she has certifications in Psychology, Hypnosis, Reiki, Bioenergetic Healing with Crystals, Angelic Healing, Dream Interpretation and is a Spiritual Instructor. Ruby has knowledge of Gemology, which she uses to program stones or minerals and turn them into powerful Amulets or Talismans of protection.

Rubi has a practical and results-oriented character, which has allowed him to have a special and integrating vision of various worlds, facilitating solutions to specific problems. Alina writes the Monthly Horoscopes for the website of the American Association of Astrologers; you can read them on the www.astrologers.com website. At this time he writes a weekly column in the newspaper El Nuevo Herald on spiritual topics, published every Sunday in digital form and on Mondays in print. He also has a program and the weekly Horoscope on the YouTube channel of this newspaper. His Astrological Yearbook is published every year in the newspaper "Diario las Américas", under the column Rubí Astrologa.

Rubi has authored several articles on astrology for the monthly publication "Today's Astrologer", has taught classes in Astrology, Tarot, Hand Reading, Crystal Healing, and Esotericism. She has weekly videos on esoteric topics on her YouTube channel: Rubi Astrologa. She had her own Astrology program broadcast daily through Flamingo T.V., she has been interviewed by several T.V. and radio programs, and every year her "Astrological Yearbook" is published with the horoscope sign by sign, and other interesting mystical topics.

She is the author of the books "Rice and Beans for the Soul" Part I, II, and III, a compilation of esoteric articles, published in English, Spanish, French, Italian, and Portuguese. "Money for All Pockets", "Love for All Hearts", "Health for All Bodies", Astrological Yearbook 2021,2022, 2023,2024, 2025, Rituals and Spells for Success in 2022, Spells and Secrets, Astrology Classes, Rituals and Amulets 2025 and Chinese Horoscope 2025 all available in five languages: English, Italian, French, Japanese and German.

Rubi speaks English and Spanish perfectly, combining all his talents and knowledge in his readings. He currently resides in Miami, Florida.

For more information you can **visit the www.esoterismomagia.com website**

Milton Keynes UK
Ingram Content Group UK Ltd.
UKHW021849231124
451423UK00001B/300